LANGUAGE

INSIDE
THE U.S.A.

PROGRAM AUTHORS

Deborah J. Short

Josefina Villamil Tinajero

NATIONAL GEOGRAPHIC   Hampton-Brown

Acknowledgments

Grateful acknowledgment is given to the authors, artists, photographers, museums, publishers, and agents for permission to reprint copyrighted material. Every effort has been made to secure the appropriate permission. If any omissions have been made or if corrections are required, please contact the Publisher.

Cover Photos
Cover, Title (tc) Digital Art/Corbis, (l-r) Todd Gipstein/Corbis, Gerald French/Corbis, Joseph Sohm/Visions of America/Corbis, Tom Grill/Corbis, Momatiuk – Eastcott/Corbis, Corbis.

Acknowledgments continue on page 330.

Published by National Geographic School Publishing & Hampton-Brown
Alison Wagner, President & Chief Executive Officer

Editorial: Alice Adamczyk, Linda Alders, Chris Beem, Lisa Berti, Sarah Chavkin, Darin Derstine, Jennifer Eckert, Amanda Gebhardt, Nadine Guarrera, Joan Johnson, Daphne Liu, Nancy Lockwood, Kathleen Maguire, Cheryl Marecki, Jim O'Neill, Susan Schaffrath, Tom Schiele, Lin Sullivan, Seija Surr, Jennifer Tetzloff, Joy Triche, Marietta Urban, Sharon Ursino, Beatrice Villar, Bill Smith Group, Brown Publishing Network, Trillium Publishing

Art, Design, and Production: Marcia Bateman, Christy Caldwell, Alex von Dallwitz, Michael Farmer, Chanté Fields, Karen Hunting, Raul Lozano, Douglas McLeod, Mary McMurtry, Marie Murphy, Marian O'Neal, Jackie Petro, Scott Russel, Donna Turner, Scott Yager, Bill Smith Group, Brown Publishing Network, Trillium Publishing

The National Geographic Society
John M. Fahey, Jr., President & Chief Executive Officer
Gilbert M. Grosvenor, Chairman of the Board

Manufacturing and Quality Management, The National Geographic Society
Christopher A. Liedel, Executive Vice President & Chief Financial Officer
George Bounelis, Vice President

National Geographic School Publishing
Hampton-Brown
www.NGSP.com

Printed in the USA
RR Donnelley, Menasha, WI

ISBN: 978-0-7362-7054-0

13 14 15 16 17 18 10 9 8 7

Program Authors

Deborah J. Short, Ph.D.
Senior Research Associate, Center for Applied Linguistics

Dr. Deborah Short is a codeveloper of the research-validated SIOP Model for directed sheltered instruction. She has directed quasi-experimental and experimental studies on English language learners funded by the Carnegie Corporation of New York, the Rockefeller Foundation, and the U.S. Department of Education. She recently chaired an expert panel on adolescent ELL literacy and coauthored a policy report: *Double the Work: Challenges and Solutions to Acquiring Language and Academic Literacy for Adolescent English Language Learners*. She has also conducted extensive research on secondary-level newcomer programs. Her research articles have appeared in *TESOL Quarterly*, *The Journal of Educational Research*, *Educational Leadership*, *Education and Urban Society*, *TESOL Journal*, and *Social Education*.

Josefina Villamil Tinajero, Ph.D.
Associate Dean, Professor of Education, University of Texas at El Paso

Dr. Josefina Villamil Tinajero specializes in staff development and school-university partnership programs, and consulted with school districts in the U.S. to design ESL, bilingual, literacy, and biliteracy programs. She has served on state and national advisory committees for standards development, including the English as a New Language Advisory Panel of the National Board of Professional Teaching Standards. She is currently Professor of Bilingual Education and Dean of the College of Education at the University of Texas at El Paso, and was President of the National Association for Bilingual Education, 1997–2000.

Nice to Meet You

Your School

Unit 3

Your School Day

Everything You Do

Unit 5

At Lunch

Unit 6

Information Everywhere

Theme Book

Bus Stop

Unit 7

How Do You Feel?

Theme Book

Word File

Unit 8

Brrr! Put On Your Coat!

Theme Book

Word File

Unit 9

Around Town

Theme Book

Word File

Unit 10

All Year Long

Unit 1

Nice to Meet You

Unit Project

Write some information about yourself on a class list. Then compare it with your friends.

In This Unit

Try Out Language	Vocabulary	Language Function	Patterns	Language Wrap-Up	Writing
Chant	Greetings and Good-byes Numbers and Number Words	Give Personal Information	*My name is _____ .* *I live at _____ .* *My phone number is _____ .*	Language Game: Got Your Name! Got Your Number!	Write About Yourself
Chant	Family Polite Words Family Words and Polite Words	Make Introductions	*_____ , this is _____ .* *Hello / Hi, _____ .* *Nice to meet you.* *Glad to meet you, too.* *Welcome, _____ .*	Theme Theater: What Do I Say?	
Song	Places in the World The United States of America	Give Information	*I am from _____ .* *Now I live in _____ .*	Read and Retell	

From Cuba to the United States

by Maritza Lopez Garcia

Theme Book

Listen and Chant

Hello and Good-bye

Hello! My name is Carlos.

Hi! My name is Mai.

See you in class!

See you soon! Good-bye!

Make your own chant. Use your own name.

after school

at lunch

Word File

GREETINGS AND GOOD-BYES

Check the words you know.

- ☐ **Good morning.**
- ☐ **Hello.**
- ☐ **Hey.**
- ☐ **Hi.**
- ☐ **Hi there.**
- ☐ **Bye.**
- ☐ **Good-bye.**
- ☐ **Have a nice day.**
- ☐ **See you later.**
- ☐ **See you soon.**

1

2

3

4

3

See you soon, Anita.

Bye, Ivan.

1

See you later.

Bye.

4

Good-bye, everyone. Have a nice day.

Good-bye, Mr. Young.

2

Good-bye.

See you later, Joe.

Word File

GREETINGS AND GOOD-BYES

Study and practice the words. Then check the words you use.

- ☐ **Good morning.**
- ☐ **Hello.**
- ☐ **Hey.**
- ☐ **Hi.**
- ☐ **Hi there.**
- ☐ **Bye.**
- ☐ **Good-bye.**
- ☐ **Have a nice day.**
- ☐ **See you later.**
- ☐ **See you soon.**

Find or draw more pictures of greetings and good-byes. Add them to your Word File.

- ☐ _____
- ☐ _____
- ☐ _____
- ☐ _____
- ☐ _____
- ☐ _____

Vocabulary

Numbers and Number Words

Say each number. Read the number words.

1	one	11	eleven	21	twenty-one		
2	two	12	twelve	22	twenty-two		
3	three	13	thirteen	23	twenty-three		
4	four	14	fourteen	24	twenty-four		
5	five	15	fifteen	25	twenty-five		
6	six	16	sixteen	26	twenty-six		
7	seven	17	seventeen	27	twenty-seven		
8	eight	18	eighteen	28	twenty-eight		
9	nine	19	nineteen	29	twenty-nine		
10	ten	20	twenty	30	thirty		

40	forty	101	one hundred one	170	one hundred seventy
50	fifty	110	one hundred ten	180	one hundred eighty
60	sixty	120	one hundred twenty	190	one hundred ninety
70	seventy	130	one hundred thirty	200	two hundred
80	eighty	140	one hundred forty	300	three hundred
90	ninety	150	one hundred fifty	1,000	one thousand
100	one hundred	160	one hundred sixty	1,000,000	one million

SCIENCE CLASSROOM 22

twenty-two

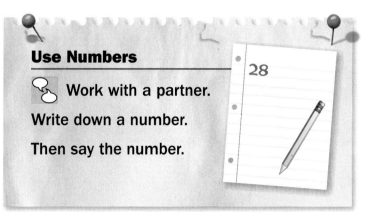

Use Numbers

Work with a partner.

Write down a number.

Then say the number.

28

© NGSP & HB

Vocabulary

Numbers and Number Words

 Look at each picture.

 Say the number.

 Then write the number in words.

WORD BANK

seven	eighty-five
twenty-three	one hundred seventy-five
forty-five	two hundred
sixty-one	

2

175

3

BONUS   POSS   PERIOD   POSS

FOULS   PLAYER FOULS

1 sixty-one

61

4

85

5 _____

6 _____

7 _____

Use Numbers and Number Words

 Work with a partner. Point to a number in your classroom. Say the number.

Give Personal Information

Listen and Say

Use these sentences to tell about yourself.

My name is _____ .	I live at _____ .	My phone number is _____ .

The School Office

Ms. Estes: Hello.

Denis: Good morning, Ms. Estes. My name is Denis.

Ms. Estes: I need your address and phone number.

Denis: I live at 155 Main Street. My phone number is 520-555-3147.

Ms. Estes: Thank you, Denis.

Denis: Good-bye, Ms. Estes. Have a nice day.

Ms. Estes: Good-bye, Denis. Have a nice day, too.

Say It Another Way

 CD 1 Track 3

Say addresses and phone numbers in a special way.

	✎ Write It	💬 Say It
Address	155 Main Street	"one fifty-five Main Street"
	5827 Main Street	"fifty-eight twenty-seven Main Street"
Phone Number	520-555-3147	"five two zero – five five five – three one four seven"

© NGSP & HB

Say and Write

Look at the names, addresses, and phone numbers.

Say the words that finish each sentence. Then write the words.

1

Denis
155 Main Street
520-555-3147

Hi. My name is _Denis_ . I live at

155 Main Street . My phone

number is _520-555-3147_ .

2

Luisa
5827 Main Street
520-555-2681

Hi. My name _____ _____ . I _live_

at _5827 Main Street_ . My phone

number _____ _____ .

3

Khalid
12 River Road
214-555-6004

Hello. My name is _____ .

I live at _____ . My phone

number is _214-555-6004_ .

4

Tonya
2136 First Street
512-555-0056

_____ . My _____ _____

_____ . I _____ _____

_____ . My _____

_____ _____ .

On Your Own

Talk to other students.
Tell them your name, address,
and phone number.

> Hi. My name is Anita. I live at
> 1421 Green Street. My phone
> number is 713-555-6943.

Language Wrap-Up

Play a Game

How to Play

1. Play with 2 to 4 players. Each player chooses a character on the game board to play.

2. Player 1 places a coin on START on the game board.

3. Player 1 throws a number cube and moves his or her coin the number of spaces on the game board.

4. Player 1 follows the instructions in the space for his or her character.

My name is
_____.

5. Players take turns.

6. The first player to reach END wins the game.

Rosa Reyes
714 Ridgewood Street
830-555-2587

Lee Kim
41 Oak Street
702-555-6340

Got Your Name! Got Your Number!

START

END

Say your name.

Lose a turn.

Say good-bye to someone.

Say hello to someone.

Say where you live.

Say your phone number.

Go back one space.

Say hello to someone.

Say where you live.

Say good-bye to someone.

Go back one space.

Say your name.

Say where you live.

Say good-bye to someone.

Say hello to someone.

Say your phone number.

Go back to START.

Say your name.

Lose a turn.

Say where you live.

Go back one space.

Say your phone number.

Say hello to someone.

Saba Ali
222 Elm Street
747-555-4017

Joe Thompson
1925 Third Street
520-555-3194

CD 1 Track 4

This Is My Family

This is my father,
And this is my mother.
This is my sister,
And this is my brother.

We are glad to meet you.
We hope you feel the same.
Please stay and talk to us.
Let's learn each other's names.

14

© NGSP & HB

Word File

FAMILY

Check the words you know.

- ☐ aunt
- ☐ niece
- ☐ brother
- ☐ cousin
- ☐ family
- ☐ father
- ☐ daughter
- ☐ grandfather
- ☐ granddaughter
- ☐ grandmother
- ☐ grandson
- ☐ mother
- ☐ son
- ☐ sister
- ☐ uncle
- ☐ nephew

5

6

7

8

9

10

11

12

13

14

This is my granddaughter.

10

This is my grandson.

11

This is my son.

12

This is my brother.

13

This is my nephew.

14

This is my niece.

5

This is my brother.

6

This is my cousin.

7

This is my family.

8

This is my daughter.

9

Word File

FAMILY
Study and practice the words. Then check the words you use.

- [ ] **aunt**
- [ ] **niece**
- [ ] **brother**
- [ ] **cousin**
- [ ] **family**
- [ ] **father**
- [ ] **daughter**
- [ ] **grandfather**
- [ ] **granddaughter**
- [ ] **grandmother**
- [ ] **grandson**
- [ ] **mother**
- [ ] **son**
- [ ] **sister**
- [ ] **uncle**
- [ ] **nephew**

Find or draw more pictures of family members. Add them to your Word File.

- [ ] _____
- [ ] _____
- [ ] _____
- [ ] _____
- [ ] _____
- [ ] _____

Polite Words

Use the word **please** when you want someone to do something.

To thank someone, say **thank you**. If someone thanks you, say **you're welcome**.

Please sit down.

Please have one.

Thank you.

You're welcome.

 Say the polite words for the pictures. Then write them.

1

_____ come in.

3 Thank you.

_____

_____

2

_____ open this.

Use Polite Words

 Look at the pictures again. Work with a partner. What other polite words can you add? Act them out.

Vocabulary

Family Words and Polite Words

 Look at the pictures in the family tree.

 Say the word for each family member.

 Then write the family words.

WORD BANK

aunt	grandmother
brother	mother
cousin	sister
father	uncle
grandfather	

1 my _____

2 my _____

3 my _____

4 my _____

5 my _____

6 my _____

7 my _____

8 my _____

9 my _____

10 my _____

11 my _____

12 _____ me

18 **Unit 1** | Nice to Meet You

© NGSP & HB

Read the speech balloons below. What does each family member say?

Write the words in each speech balloon.

Please take this gift, Aunt Fong.

You're welcome, Aunt Fong.

Thank you.

1

_____ _____ _____

_____ _____ _____

2

_____ _____

_____ _____

Use Family Words and Polite Words

Work with a partner. Act out the scene.

Make Introductions

Listen and Say

Use words and sentences like these when you introduce or meet people.

INTRODUCTION	RESPONSES		
_____ , this is _____ .	Hello, _____ . Hi, _____ .	Nice to meet you.	Glad to meet you, too.

This Is Katie

Maya: Amy, this is Katie.
Katie, this is my friend Amy.

Amy: Hi, Katie. Nice to meet you.

Katie: Glad to meet you, too.

Say It Another Way

CD 1 Track 6

People use different ways to make introductions.

Ways to Introduce People	Ways to Respond	More Things to Say
This is Katie. I want you to meet Katie. I would like you to meet Katie.	Nice to meet you. Glad to meet you. It's a pleasure to meet you.	

More Things to Say photo: How are you? I'm fine. Thank you.

Say and Write

 Read the speech balloons below.

 What does each person say? Write the words in each speech balloon.

Nice to meet you.	Hello, Mrs. Walker. This is my friend Carlos.	Welcome, Carlos. Glad to meet you, too.	Carlos, this is Mrs. Walker.

On Your Own

Work with two partners. Act out the scene.

Language Wrap-Up

Theme Theater

Yuen and his family are having a party. His good friend
Eric is there. Listen to their conversation. Then act it out.

WHAT DO I SAY?

YUEN: My Aunt Ying is coming to the party.
I will meet her today.
What will I say to her?

CHORUS: *Yuen will meet his aunt today.*
What will he say?
What will he say?

ERIC: Say hello to her.
Say you are glad to see her.

YUEN: Then what do I say?

ERIC: Then introduce yourself.

◊   ◊   ◊

[Aunt Ying arrives.]

CHORUS: *What will Yuen say?*
Do you know?
Eric tells Yuen to say hello.

YUEN: Hello, Aunt Ying. Please come in.
My name is Yuen.

AUNT YING: Hello, nephew. I am glad to
see you. You are so tall!

YUEN: Aunt Ying, this is my friend Eric. Eric, this is my aunt, Aunt Ying.

ERIC: Hello, Aunt Ying. Nice to meet you.

AUNT YING: Hi, Eric. Glad to meet you, too!

ERIC: I have my camera. May I please take your picture?

YUEN: Yes! Thank you!

CHORUS: *Eric is a very good friend.*
He takes a picture of Aunt Ying and Yuen.

CD 1 Track 8
Tune: "Hello Mother, Hello Father"

Listen and Sing

Let's Be Friends

I am Pablo. I'm from Cuba.

I live in Flagstaff, Arizona.

I'd like to meet you and get to know you.

We Cubans are a friendly bunch if I may show you.

I am Tanya. I'm from Russia.

I live in Stockton, California.

Yes, I've heard that you are friendly

From Mei Ling, Marta, Mariluz, and my friend Kim-Ly!

Make your own song with a partner. Use your own name, home country, and place where you live.

© NGSP & HB

Word File

PLACES IN THE WORLD

Check the words you know. Draw your country on the blank card.

- ☐ China
- ☐ Colombia
- ☐ Cuba
- ☐ Dominican Republic
- ☐ El Salvador
- ☐ Ethiopia
- ☐ Guatemala
- ☐ Haiti
- ☐ India
- ☐ Iran
- ☐ Jamaica
- ☐ Mexico
- ☐ Pakistan
- ☐ Peru
- ☐ Philippines
- ☐ Russia
- ☐ South Korea
- ☐ Vietnam

15

China

16

Colombia

17

Cuba

18

Dominican Republic

19

El Salvador

20

Ethiopia

21

Guatemala

22

Haiti

23

India

24

20 Iran

15 Peru

21 Jamaica

16 Philippines

22 Mexico

17 Russia

23 Pakistan

18 South Korea

24

19 Vietnam

Word File

PLACES IN THE WORLD

Study and practice the words. Then check the words you use.

- [ ] **China**
- [ ] **Colombia**
- [ ] **Cuba**
- [ ] **Dominican Republic**
- [ ] **El Salvador**
- [ ] **Ethiopia**
- [ ] **Guatemala**
- [ ] **Haiti**
- [ ] **India**
- [ ] **Iran**
- [ ] **Jamaica**
- [ ] **Mexico**
- [ ] **Pakistan**
- [ ] **Peru**
- [ ] **Philippines**
- [ ] **Russia**
- [ ] **South Korea**
- [ ] **Vietnam**

Find or draw more pictures of places in the world. Add them to your Word File.

- [ ] _____
- [ ] _____
- [ ] _____
- [ ] _____
- [ ] _____
- [ ] _____

The United States of America

 Look at the map.   Say the name of each state. Color in your state.

New Hampshire
Vermont
Massachusetts
Michigan
Indiana
Maine
New York
Pennsylvania
Rhode Island
Connecticut
New Jersey
Delaware
Maryland
Washington D.C.
West Virginia
North Carolina
South Carolina
Florida

Washington
Montana
North Dakota
Minnesota
Wisconsin
Oregon
Idaho
South Dakota
Iowa
Wyoming
Nebraska
Illinois
Ohio
Nevada
Utah
Colorado
Kansas
Missouri
Kentucky
Virginia
California
Arizona
Oklahoma
Tennessee
New Mexico
Georgia
Texas
Alabama
Mississippi
Louisiana
Arkansas
Alaska
Hawaii

★ = capital of the United States

Name the States

 Work with a partner. Point to a state on the map. Say the name of that state.

Give Information

Listen and Say

Use these sentences to talk about yourself.

| I am from _____ . | Now I live in _____ . |

1

"I am from Mexico.
Now I live in Texas."

2

"I am from Pakistan.
Now I live in New York."

3

"I am from Jamaica.
Now I live in California."

Say It Another Way

 CD 1 Track 10

When you talk about yourself, use **I am** or **I'm**.

I am	I'm
I am from Mexico.	I'm from Mexico.
I am from Pakistan.	I'm from Pakistan.
I am from Jamaica.	I'm from Jamaica.

Shorten the two words like this:

Add '

I am = I'm

Take out a letter.

Say and Write

  Look at each picture. Say the words that finish each sentence.

Then write the words.

4

Russia

New York

I am from <u>Russia</u> .

Now I live in <u>New York</u> .

6

Ethiopia

Minnesota

I <u>am</u> _____

_____ .

Now I _____ _____

_____ .

8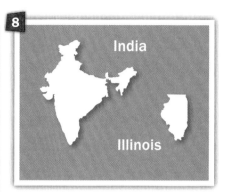

India

Illinois

I'm from _____ .

_____ _____ _____

_____ _____ _____ .

5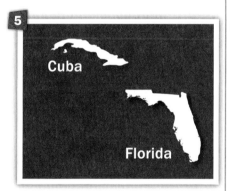

Cuba

Florida

I am from _____ .

Now I live in _____ .

7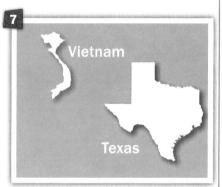

Vietnam

Texas

I _____ _____

_____ .

Now _____ _____ _____

_____ .

9

Mexico

Nevada

_____ _____

_____ .

_____ _____

_____ _____ .

On Your Own

 Work with a partner.

Show a picture of your country.

Introduce yourself.

Hi. My name is Alexei.
I am from Russia.
Now I live in New York.
I live at 456 Maple Street.

Language Wrap-Up

Read and Retell

Build Background

Now you will read *From Cuba to the United States*. Maritza just moved to the United States from Cuba.

Read

As you read, find out what Maritza learns about her new home.

Collect Words

You know many words for family. Write some of the words. Use the words to talk about the book.

Theme Book
CD 1 Track 11

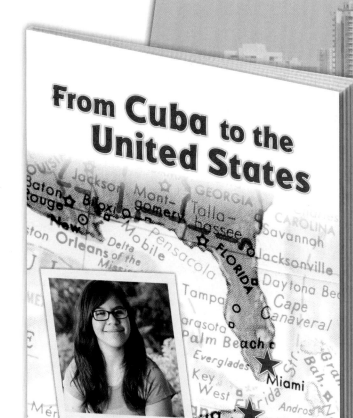

From Cuba to the United States

by Maritza Lopez Garcia

Word Web

father

Family

Tell About the Book

1 Think about Maritza's life in Cuba. Write about people and things she had there.

	Matanzas, Cuba	Miami, Florida, U.S.A.
Family	father, mother, brothers	
Friends		
Home		
Food		

2 Now think about Maritza's life in Miami. Write about people and things she has there. Finish the chart.

3 Use your chart to tell a partner about Maritza's life in Cuba and in the United States.

Write About Yourself

Study a Model

Hi. I am Rogelio Vargas.
I am from Mexico.
Now I live in Chicago, Illinois.
I am glad to meet you!

At home in Mexico

At home in Chicago

Focus on Sentences

Some sentences tell something. They end with a **period**.

I am from Mexico. < **period**

Start every sentence with a capital letter. Always capitalize the word **I**.

Now I live in Chicago, Illinois.

capital letters

✐ Write each sentence. Use capital letters and periods.

1 now i live here _____

2 i live with my family _____

3 my phone number is 828-555-2323

_____

Letters	
lowercase	
capital > Aa	Nn
Bb	Oo
Cc	Pp
Dd	Qq
Ee	Rr
Ff	Ss
Gg	Tt
Hh	Uu
Ii	Vv
Jj	Ww
Kk	Xx
Ll	Yy
Mm	Zz

Write about yourself. Draw pictures or tape some photos of yourself to this page.

Share your work with a partner. Check the writing. Do you need to add a period to the end of a sentence? Do you need to add any capital letters?

Unit 2

Your School

Unit Project

Tell about your school in your home country.

In This Unit

Try Out Language	Vocabulary	Language Function	Patterns	Language Wrap-Up	Writing
Chant	School Tools Colors and Sizes	Give Information Ask and Answer Questions	*This is _____ .* *Here is _____ .* *I have _____ .* *It is _____ .* *Is this _____ ?* *Yes, it is.* *No, it is not. It's _____ .* *No, it isn't. It's _____ .*	Language Game: What Is It?	Write About Your Schools
Chant	In the Classroom Shapes	Give and Follow Commands	*Show me _____ .* *Point to _____ .*	Theme Theater: The First Day of School	
Song	School Places School Places and Things	Ask and Answer Questions	*What is in the _____ ?* *A _____ is in the _____ .* *What is on the _____ ?* *A _____ is on the _____ .*	Read and Retell **Cool Schools**	

Theme Book

Listen and Chant

Cool Tools

Use **a pen** when you're at school.
Using tools is really cool!

Use **a ruler** when you're at school.
Using tools is really cool!

Make your own chant.

a stapler

a book

a calculator

a notebook

a pencil

© NGSP & HB

SCHOOL TOOLS

Check the words you know.

- ☐ a book
- ☐ a calculator
- ☐ a key
- ☐ an eraser
- ☐ a notebook
- ☐ a pair of scissors
- ☐ a pen
- ☐ a pencil
- ☐ a piece of paper
- ☐ a ruler
- ☐ a stapler

25

26

27

28

29

30

31

32

33

34

30 a pen

25 a book

31 an eraser / a pencil

26 a key / a calculator

32 a piece of paper

27 an eraser

33 a ruler

28 a notebook

34 a stapler

29 a pair of scissors

Word File

SCHOOL TOOLS

Study and practice the words. Then check the words you use.

- ☐ **a book**
- ☐ **a calculator**
- ☐ **a key**
- ☐ **an eraser**
- ☐ **a notebook**
- ☐ **a pair of scissors**
- ☐ **a pen**
- ☐ **a pencil**
- ☐ **a piece of paper**
- ☐ **a ruler**
- ☐ **a stapler**

Find or draw more pictures of tools you use in school. Add them to your Word File.

- ☐ _____
- ☐ _____
- ☐ _____
- ☐ _____
- ☐ _____
- ☐ _____

© NGSP & HB

Colors and Sizes

Use these words for colors and sizes.

Colors

yellow	orange	red	pink	green	blue

purple	brown	black	gray	white

a **red** pen

Sizes

a **big** notebook   a **little** notebook   a **long** pencil   a **short** pencil

👓 Look at each picture. 💬 Say the words. ✍️ Then write the words.

1 a <u>long</u> pencil

2 a short _____

3 a _____ _____

4 a _____ _____

Use Color and Size Words

🗣 Work with a partner.
Show a picture of a school tool. Talk about each picture.

© NGSP & HB

Vocabulary

School Tools, Colors, and Sizes

 Look at each picture.

 Say the name of each tool.

Say its color or size.

 Then write about the tool.

WORD BANK

a book	black	big
a calculator	blue	little
an eraser	brown	long
a pair of scissors	gray	short
a pen	green	
a pencil	orange	
a piece of paper	red	
a ruler	white	
a stapler	yellow	

1

a ___little___ ___eraser___

2

a _____ _____

3

a _____ _____

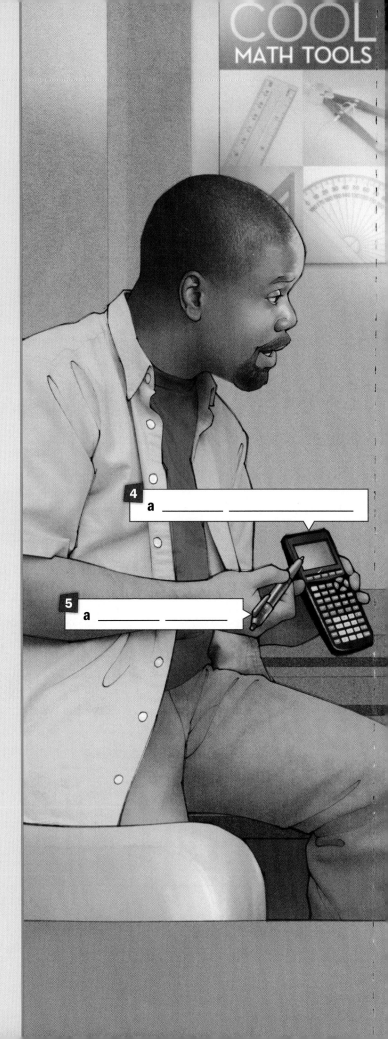

COOL MATH TOOLS

4 a _____ _____

5 a _____ _____

Give Information

Listen and Say

Use sentences like these to tell about things in your classroom.

| This is _____ . | Here is _____ . | I have _____ . |
| It is _____ . | It is _____ . | It is _____ . |

"This is a ruler. It is long."

"Here is an eraser. It is green."

"I have a notebook. It is big."

Use the Right Word

a	an
Use **a** if the next word starts with a consonant sound.	Use **an** if the next word starts with a vowel sound.
a <u>b</u>ook a <u>n</u>otebook a <u>p</u>encil	**an** <u>e</u>raser
Consonants: b, c, d, f, g, h, j, k, l, m, n, p, q, r, s, t, v, w, x, y, z	**Vowels:** a, e, i, o, u

Say and Write

  Look at each picture. Say the words that finish each sentence.

Then write the words.

4

This is a ___book___ .

It is ___little___ .

5

This is ___a___ _____ .

It ____ _____ .

6

Here is ____ _____ .

It is _____ .

7

Here ____ ____ _____ .

____ ____ _____ .

8

I have ____ _____ .

It ____ _____ .

9

I _____ ____ _____ .

It ____ _____ .

On Your Own

Work with a partner. Talk about the tools you use in school. Tell about their colors and sizes.

> This is a notebook.
> It is green.

Ask and Answer Questions

Listen and Say

Use questions like these to find out the names of things.

Is this _____ ?	Is this _____ ?	Is this _____ ?
Yes, it is.	No, it is not.	No, it is not. It's _____ .
	No, it isn't.	No, it isn't. It's _____ .

1 "Is this a pen?" "Yes, it is."

2 "Is this a pen?" "No, it is not."

3 "Is this a stapler?" "No, it isn't. It's a ruler."

How It Works

Ask a question to get information.

A question starts with a **capital letter** and ends with a **question mark**.

capital letter
"**I**s this a pen**?**"
question mark

Answer questions like these with **yes** or **no**.

Say and Write

  Look at each picture. Say the words that finish each question and answer.
Then write the words.

4

__Is__ this a calculator?

Yes, it is.

6

____ ____ ____ notebook?

No, ____ ____ _____ .

It's a _____ .

8

____ ____ ____ eraser?

_____ , ____ ____ .

5

____ ____ a ruler?

No, it is not. It's a

___pen___ .

7

____ ____ ____ pen?

No, ____ isn't.

It's ____ _____ .

9

____ ____ ____ pair of

scissors?

No, ____ _____ .

On Your Own

Work with a partner. Ask questions about the
tools you use in school. Answer the questions with
Yes, it is or *No, it isn't. It's* ____ .

Is this a ruler?

No, it isn't.
It's a stapler.

Language Wrap-Up

Play a Game

How to Play

1. Play with a partner.

2. Make a spinner with a paper clip.
Hold it in the center of the circle with a pencil.

3. Partner 1 spins and asks a question.

> Is this a pencil?

> Is this an eraser?

4. Partner 2 answers.

> Yes, it is.

> No, it isn't. It's _____ .

5. Then Partner 2 spins.

What Is It?

Listen and Chant

In the Classroom

Here is a desk. Here is a chair.

Here are students everywhere.

Make your own chant.

bookcase

table

map

clock

Word File

IN THE CLASSROOM
Check the words
you know.

- [ ] **board**
- [ ] **bookcase**
- [ ] **chair**
- [ ] **clock**
- [ ] **computer**
- [ ] **desk**
- [ ] **map**
- [ ] **student**
- [ ] **table**
- [ ] **teacher**

35

36

37

38

39

40

41

42

43

44

desk

40

map

41

student

42

table

43

teacher

44

board

35

bookcase

36

chair

37

clock

38

computer

39

Word File

IN THE CLASSROOM
Study and practice the words. Then check the words you use.

- ☐ **board**
- ☐ **bookcase**
- ☐ **chair**
- ☐ **clock**
- ☐ **computer**
- ☐ **desk**
- ☐ **map**
- ☐ **student**
- ☐ **table**
- ☐ **teacher**

Find or draw more pictures of things in a classroom. Add them to your Word File.

- ☐ _____
- ☐ _____
- ☐ _____
- ☐ _____
- ☐ _____
- ☐ _____

© NGSP & HB

Shapes

Here are the names of four shapes.

circle

triangle

rectangle

square

 Look at each thing. **Write the shape.**

1 The piece of paper

is a _rectangle_ .

2 The clock

is a _____ .

3 The table

is a _____ .

4 The map

is a _____ .

5 The ruler

is a _____ .

6 The bookcase

is a _____ .

7 The piece of paper

is a _____ .

Name More Shapes

Work with a partner. Find things in your classroom for each shape.

Draw a picture on a card. Your partner names the shape.

Vocabulary

In the Classroom

 Look at each picture.

 Say the name of the item.

 Then write the name.

WORD BANK

board	desk
bookcase	map
chair	student
clock	table
computer	teacher

1. board

2.

3.

4.

5.

6

_____

7

_____

8

_____

10

9

Guess the Object

Work with a partner. Find things in your classroom. Tell the size, color, and shape. Your partner names the thing.

It is big. It is brown. It is a rectangle.

A table!

Give and Follow Commands

Listen and Say

Use words like these to give a command.

| Show me _____ . | Point to _____ . |

1 Show me a pen.

3 Point to the board.

2 Show me a ruler.

4 Point to a chair.

Use the Right Word

a	the
Use **a** to talk about one thing that is not specific.	Use **the** to talk about a specific thing.
Point to **a** book.	Point to **the** book on my desk.

Say and Point

💬 Say each command. Your partner points to the object in the picture.

5 Point to a map.

6 Show me a circle.

7 Show me a chair.

8 Point to a desk.

9 Point to a rectangle.

10 Point to the teacher.

11 Show me a student.

12 Show me a book.

13 Show me a table.

On Your Own

 Take turns with a partner.

Give commands and follow commands.

Use things in the classroom.

Show me a pen.

Theme Theater

Today is Miguel and Gloria's first day of school. Listen to their conversation. Then act it out.

THE FIRST DAY OF SCHOOL

MIGUEL: This is our new classroom. Look at that map, Gloria!

GLORIA: It is big!

MRS. JONES: Hello, students. I am Mrs. Jones. I am your new teacher.

MIGUEL: Hi. My name is Miguel.

GLORIA: Hello. My name is Gloria.

◇   ◇   ◇

CHORUS	MRS. JONES	GLORIA	MIGUEL

MIGUEL: Can you show us the classoom, please?

MRS. JONES: Yes. Here are your desks and chairs. Here is a bookcase.

GLORIA: Do you have a computer?

MRS. JONES: Yes. Here is the computer. Everyone shares it.

CHORUS: *Here is a desk.*
Here is a chair.
Here is the computer
for students to share.

◊   ◊   ◊

MRS. JONES: Do you have everything you need for the class?

MIGUEL: I think so. I have a pen, a pencil, and a notebook.

GLORIA: I do, too. I also have a ruler and a calculator.

CHORUS: *Miguel has a pen, a pencil,*
and a notebook.
Gloria has a ruler and
a calculator.

[Other students walk into the room.
The bell rings.]

MRS. JONES: Hello, everyone. Please sit down.

Try Out Language

Listen and Sing

WHAT'S IN
OUR SCHOOL?

What's in our |school|?
What's in our |school|?
Do you know what is in
our |school|?

Look over there.
I *see* a |gym|.
A |gym| is in our |school|.

Make your own song.

gym

window

classroom

map

© NGSP & HB

Word File

SCHOOL PLACES
Check the words you know.

- [ ] **main building**
- [ ] **door**
- [ ] **entrance**
- [ ] **gym**
- [ ] **fence**
- [ ] **flag**
- [ ] **flagpole**
- [ ] **steps**
- [ ] **window**
- [ ] **field**
- [ ] **track**

45

50

46

51

47

52

48

53

49

54

50 flag / flagpole

51 steps

52 window

53 field

54 track

45 main building

46 401 PRINCIPAL'S OFFICE / door

47 entrance

48 gym

49 fence

Word File

SCHOOL PLACES

Study and practice the words. Then check the words you use.

- [ ] **main building**
- [ ] **door**
- [ ] **entrance**
- [ ] **gym**
- [ ] **fence**
- [ ] **flag**
- [ ] **flagpole**
- [ ] **steps**
- [ ] **window**
- [ ] **field**
- [ ] **track**

Find or draw more pictures of school places. Add them to your Word File.

- [ ] _____
- [ ] _____
- [ ] _____
- [ ] _____
- [ ] _____
- [ ] _____

Word File

SCHOOL PLACES AND THINGS

Check the words you know.

- [ ] cafeteria
- [ ] fork
- [ ] knife
- [ ] spoon
- [ ] line
- [ ] bathroom
- [ ] paper towel
- [ ] money
- [ ] napkin
- [ ] plate
- [ ] tray
- [ ] sink
- [ ] soap
- [ ] water
- [ ] toilet

55

56

57

58

59

60

61

62

63

64

60 money

61 napkin

62 tray plate

63 soap sink water

64 toilet

55 cafeteria

56 spoon fork knife

57 line

58 bathroom

59 paper towel

Word File

SCHOOL PLACES AND THINGS

Study and practice the words. Then check the words you use.

- ☐ cafeteria
- ☐ fork
- ☐ knife
- ☐ spoon
- ☐ line
- ☐ bathroom
- ☐ paper towel
- ☐ money
- ☐ napkin
- ☐ plate
- ☐ tray
- ☐ sink
- ☐ soap
- ☐ water
- ☐ toilet

Find or draw more pictures of school places. Add them to your Word File.

- ☐ _____
- ☐ _____
- ☐ _____
- ☐ _____
- ☐ _____
- ☐ _____

Vocabulary

School Places

👓 Look at each picture.

💬 Say the name of each place or thing.

✍ Then write the name.

WORD BANK	
door	flagpole
entrance	main building
fence	steps
field	track
flag	window

1

This is the ___main building___ .

2

3

8

9

10

4

5

6

7

Use School Words

💬 Work with a partner. Point to each place or thing. Say the name of each place or thing.

Vocabulary: School Places **63**

Vocabulary

School Places and Things

👓 Look at each picture.

💬 Say the name of each place or thing.

✍️ Then write the name.

WORD BANK

bathroom	money	soap
cafeteria	napkin	spoon
fork	paper towel	toilet
knife	plate	tray
line	sink	water

1

This is the _____cafeteria_____ .

© NGSP & HB

10

This is the _____ .

11

12

13

14

15

Use School Words

Work with a partner. Look at pages 64 and 65. Point to each place or thing. Say the name of each place or thing.

Ask and Answer Questions

Listen and Say

Use sentences like these to talk about where things are.

QUESTIONS	ANSWERS
What is in the _____ ?	A _____ is in the _____ .
What is on the _____ ?	A _____ is on the _____ .

1 "What is in the classroom?" "A desk is in the classroom."

2 "What is on the desk?" "A book is on the desk."

Use the Right Word

Use **in** and **on** to tell where things are.

in	on
Use **in** for a place or a thing that is inside something.	Use **on** for a place or a thing that is on top of something.

in

A map is **in** the classroom.
A board is **in** the classroom.
The classroom is **in** the school.

 on

A plate is **on** the tray.
An apple is **on** the tray.
A sandwich is **on** the plate.

Say and Write

 Look at each picture. Say the words that finish each question and answer. Then write the words.

3

What is in the __bathroom__ ?

A __sink__ is __in__ the bathroom.

5

What is _____ the

_____ ? A _____ is on

the _____ .

7

What is _____

the _____ ?

A _____ is

_____ the _____ .

4

What is __on__ the

__tray__ ? A _____ is on

the _____ .

6

What is _____ the

classroom ? A _____

is _____ the

_____ .

8

What is _____ the

_____ ?

A _____

is _____ the

_____ .

On Your Own

 Work with a partner. Look around your classroom. Ask and answer questions with *in* or *on*.

What is on the table?

A computer is on the table.

Language Wrap-Up

Read and Retell

Build Background

Now you will read *Cool Schools*. It is about different kinds of schools.

Read

As you read, learn about what you can learn in different schools.

Collect Words

You know many words about school. What new words did you learn in this book? Write the words. Use the words to talk about the book.

Cool Schools

by Louise Franklin

Theme Book

CD 1 Track 20

Word Web

globe

School Words

Tell About the Book

1 Think about the book. What is it mainly about?

Different Kinds of Schools

2 What kinds of schools does the book describe? Add sections to the map. Write the school inside each section.

high school

Different Kinds of Schools

3 Write words around each school. Tell what kinds of things you learn there.

science

high school

Different Kinds of Schools

4 Now make your own concept map. Use your completed map to tell a partner about *Cool Schools.*

Write About Your Schools

My Schools
by Inez Gonzales

Here is my school in
Monterrey, Mexico.

Here is my school in
Dallas, Texas.

My school in Monterrey

My school in Dallas

Focus on Capital Letters

Remember to start every sentence with a
capital letter.

Here is my school.

capital letter

Start the names of cities, states, and
countries with a **capital letter,** too.

capital letters

I am from **M**onterrey, **M**exico.
Now I live in **D**allas, **T**exas.

Write each sentence with capital
letters.

1 this is my school.

_____

2 i live in miami, florida.

_____

3 i am from vietnam.

_____

70

© NGSP & HB

Write about your schools. Draw pictures or tape some photos on this page. Label your pictures.

My Schools

by _____

Here is my school in

_____

_____

_____ .

_____

_____

Here is my school in

_____

_____

_____ .

_____

Share your work with a partner. Check the writing.

Use a capital letter for the first word of a sentence.

Use capital letters for the names of cities, states, or countries.

Unit 3

Your School Day

Unit Project

Create a book with pictures of the people and places in your school.

In This Unit

Try Out Language	Vocabulary	Language Function	Patterns	Language Wrap-Up	Writing
Chant	Times and Days of the Week Telling Time	Ask and Answer Questions	*What time is it?* *What day is it?* *It is _____ .* *It's _____ .*	**Language Game:** What Day Is It? What Time Is It?	Write About Your First Day in the U.S.A.
Song	School Subjects Class Schedule	Ask and Answer Questions	*When is _____ ?* *It's at _____ .* *Where is _____ ?* *It's in _____ .*	**Theme Theater:** Up Too Late	
Chant	School Places and Workers	Ask and Answer Questions Ask and Answer Questions	*Where is _____ ?* *Here it is.* *Who is the _____ ?* *_____ is the _____ .* *Who is _____ ?* *_____ is the _____ .*	**Read and Retell** Alexei's Week by Antonia Barber **Theme Book**	

Listen and Chant

WHAT TIME IS IT?

What time is it?
What time is it?

It's one o'clock in the afternoon.

I have to meet my friend in class.

Oh, that's very soon!

Make your own chant.

twelve thirty

two o'clock

three o'clock

© NGSP & HB

Word File

TIMES AND DAYS OF THE WEEK

Check the words you know.

- ☐ morning
- ☐ afternoon
- ☐ night
- ☐ noon
- ☐ evening
- ☐ day
- ☐ week

65

68

66

69

67

70

Today Is
4
Monday,
January 4

☀ January ☀						
Sunday	Monday	Tuesday	Wednesday	Thursday	Friday	Saturday

68 noon

65 morning

69 evening

66 afternoon

70

Today Is
4
Monday,
January 4

day

67 night

✳ January ✳ ✳

Sunday	Monday	Tuesday	Wednesday	Thursday	Friday	Saturday

week

TIMES AND DAYS OF THE WEEK

Study and practice the words. Then check the words you use.

- ☐ **morning**
- ☐ **afternoon**
- ☐ **night**
- ☐ **noon**
- ☐ **evening**
- ☐ **day**
- ☐ **week**

Find or draw more pictures of times and days. Add them to your Word File.

- ☐ _____
- ☐ _____
- ☐ _____
- ☐ _____
- ☐ _____
- ☐ _____

Telling Time

Use numbers or words to tell the time.

Write:	9:00	10:15	11:30	12:00	12:45	1:10	2:40
Say:	nine o'clock	ten fifteen	eleven thirty	twelve o'clock	twelve forty-five	one ten	two forty
Or say:		a quarter past ten	half past eleven	noon (or midnight)	a quarter to one	ten after one	twenty to three

Look at the time on each clock. Write the time. Then say the time.

1

8:00

3

_____

5

_____

2

_____

4

_____

Tell Time

 Tell a partner the time in each picture.

eight o'clock

Vocabulary

What Time Is It?

 Look at each picture. **Say the time.** **Then write the time of day.**

1   12:00

noon

5

_____

2   6:10

evening

6

_____

3 6:45

_____

7

_____

4 3:00

_____

8

_____

What Day Is It?

✍ Write a day on each red line. Give your book to a partner. Your partner writes a day on each green line.

✳ January ✳

Sunday	Monday	Tuesday	Wednesday	Thursday	Friday	Saturday

1

Today is ___Saturday___ .

Tomorrow is ___Sunday___ .

2

Today is _____ .

Tomorrow is _____ .

3

Today is _____ .

Tomorrow is _____ .

4

Today is _____ .

Tomorrow is _____ .

5

Today is _____ .

Tomorrow is _____ .

6

Today is _____ .

Tomorrow is _____ .

7

Today is _____ .

Tomorrow is _____ .

Tell a Day and Time

💬 Work with a partner. Say a day and a time. ✍ Your partner will draw a picture of what he or she does then.

Ask and Answer Questions

CD 1 Track 22

Listen and Say

Use questions like these to find out the time and the day.

QUESTIONS	ANSWERS	
What time is it?	It is _____ .	It's _____ .
What day is it?	It is _____ .	It's _____ .

1 | What time is it?   It is 10:00.

2 | What time is it?   It's 5:30.

3 | What day is it?   It is Monday.

4 | What day is it?   It's Friday.

Say It Another Way

CD 1 Track 23

People use different ways to ask for the time.

Ask for the Time	Tell the Time
What's the time?	It's six ten.
Do you have the time?	Yes, it's six ten.
What time do you have?	I have six ten.
Can you please tell me the time?	Yes, my watch says six ten.

Say and Write

  Look at each picture. Say the words that finish each question and answer.

Then write the words.

5

What time is it?

____It____ ____is____ 5:15.

6

What time _____ _____ ?

It _____ _____ .

7

What _____ _____ _____ ?

_____ _____ _____ .

8

What day is it?

____It____ ____is____ Tuesday.

9

What day _____ _____ ?

It _____ _____ .

10

_____ _____ _____ _____ ?

_____ _____ _____ .

On Your Own

 Write a day and draw a time on a card.

Show your card to others. Ask questions

about the day and the time.

What day is it?
What time is it?

Language Wrap-Up

Play a Game

How to Play

1. Play with a partner.

2. Partner 1 tosses a coin onto the game board to make it land on a day. Then Partner 1 asks about the day.

Thursday

> What day is it?

3. Partner 2 answers.

> It is Thursday.

4. Partner 1 tosses a coin onto the game board to make it land on a time. Partner 1 asks about the time.

> What time is it?

5. Partner 2 answers.

> It's two thirty.

6. Partners take turns.

What Day Is It?

| Sunday | Monday | Tuesday | Wednesday | Thursday | Friday | Saturday |

What Time Is It?

Try Out Language

Listen and Sing

My Schedule

I am going to science class soon.

I am going to science class soon.

When I'm done with science class,

It's time for social studies class.

Then I will eat my lunch around noon.

Make your own song.

math class

language arts class

ESL class

Hi. My name is Juan.

© NGSP & HB

SCHOOL SUBJECTS

Check the words you know. Draw two more classes on the blank cards.

- ☐ **ESL class**
- ☐ **homeroom**
- ☐ **language arts class**
- ☐ **lunch**
- ☐ **math class**
- ☐ **P.E.**
- ☐ **science class**
- ☐ **social studies class**

71

72

73

74

75

76

77

78

79

80

76 math class

77 P.E.

78 science class

79 social studies class

80

71 ESL class

72 homeroom

73 language arts class

74 lunch

75

SCHOOL SUBJECTS
Study and practice the words. Then check the words you use.

☐ **ESL class**

☐ **homeroom**

☐ **language arts class**

☐ **lunch**

☐ **math class**

☐ **P.E.**

☐ **science class**

☐ **social studies class**

Find or draw more pictures of school subjects. Add them to your Word File.

☐ _____

☐ _____

☐ _____

☐ _____

☐ _____

☐ _____

Class Schedule

Write your class schedule in this chart.

WORD BANK

ESL class   lunch   science class
homeroom   math class   social studies
language arts class   P.E.   class

_____'s Class Schedule

Class	Time	Room

Talk About Your Schedule

Work with a partner. Ask your partner about his or her class schedule. Your partner will say the time of each class.

What time is _____ ?   It's at _____ .

Ask and Answer Questions

Listen and Say

Use questions like these to find out the time and place of your classes.

QUESTIONS	ANSWERS
When is _____ ?	It's at _____ .
Where is _____ ?	It's in _____ .

1

When is ESL class?

It's at nine o'clock in the morning.

2

Where is ESL class?

It's in Room 108.

Use the Right Word

Use **at** and **in** to talk about times and places.

	at	in
Times	at 10:00 at lunch at night	in the morning in the afternoon in the evening
Places	at school at home	in the gym in Room 105

© NGSP & HB

Say and Write

 Look at the schedule. 🗨 Say the words that finish each question and answer.

✍ Then write the words.

Class	Time	Room
homeroom	8:15	110
ESL class	9:00	108
math class	9:45	124
social studies class	10:30	115
science class	11:15	122
lunch	12:00	cafeteria
language arts class	12:45	106
P.E.	1:30	gym

3

When is ___ESL class___ ?

It's at ___9:00___ .

4

When is ___science class___ ?

It's ___ ___ .

5

When is lunch?

It's ___ ___ .

6

Where is ___P.E.___ ?

It's in the ___ .

7

Where is math class?

It's ___ ___ .

8

___ is social studies class?

It's in ___ .

On Your Own

 Work with a partner. Ask questions about

your partner's class schedule on page 87. Your partner answers.

When is language arts class?

Theme Theater

Monique is studying for a science test. She is talking to her brother. Listen to their conversation. Then act it out.

UP TOO LATE

ALFRED: What are you doing, Monique? It's ten o'clock at night.

MONIQUE: I am studying. I have a science test on Wednesday.

CHORUS: *Monique has a test in science class. She is studying.*

[It is the next morning.]

ALFRED: Monique! Wake up!

MONIQUE: *[confused]* What? What time is it?

ALFRED: It's seven thirty in the morning.

MONIQUE: I'm tired. I studied all night.

ALFRED: Get ready for school now!

CHORUS: *Monique is tired. She studied all night.*

CHORUS

MRS. SOTO

MONIQUE

ALFRED

[Monique walks into her science class.]

MRS. SOTO: Monique, you are in the wrong class.

MONIQUE: I am? What day is it?

MRS. SOTO: It's Tuesday. You have science class on Wednesday.

MONIQUE: Oh. I forgot the day. Thank you, Mrs. Soto.

CHORUS: *Monique is tired. She forgot the day.*

◊   ◊   ◊

[It is Tuesday night.]

ALFRED: Did you study for your science test tomorrow?

MONIQUE: Yes, I did. What time is it?

ALFRED: Only eight o'clock.

MONIQUE: I'm going to bed. I need to sleep.

ALFRED: Good night. Good luck tomorrow.

MONIQUE: Thanks. Good night.

Where Is the LIBRARY?

Where is the library?
Do you know?
Can you show me
Where to go?

Yes, of course,
I know where.
Follow me.
I'll take you there.

Make your own chant.

nurse's office

main office

gym

cafeteria

© NGSP & HB

Word File

SCHOOL PLACES AND WORKERS

Check the words you know.

- [ ] auditorium
- [ ] students
- [ ] cafeteria
- [ ] janitor
- [ ] classroom
- [ ] teacher
- [ ] counselor's office
- [ ] counselor
- [ ] gym
- [ ] coach
- [ ] hallway
- [ ] assistant principal
- [ ] library
- [ ] librarian
- [ ] main office
- [ ] principal
- [ ] secretary
- [ ] nurse's office
- [ ] nurse
- [ ] parking lot
- [ ] bus driver

81

82

83

84

85

86

87

88

89

90

assistant principal

86 **hallway**

librarian

87 **library**

principal

secretary

88 **main office**

nurse

89 **nurse's office**

bus driver

B-57-92

90 **parking lot**

students

81 **auditorium**

janitor

82 **cafeteria**

teacher

83 **classroom**

counselor

84 **counselor's office**

coach

85 **gym**

Word File

SCHOOL PLACES AND WORKERS

Study and practice the words. Then check the words you use.

- ☐ **auditorium**
- ☐ **students**
- ☐ **cafeteria**
- ☐ **janitor**
- ☐ **classroom**
- ☐ **teacher**
- ☐ **counselor's office**
- ☐ **counselor**
- ☐ **gym**
- ☐ **coach**
- ☐ **hallway**
- ☐ **assistant principal**
- ☐ **library**
- ☐ **librarian**
- ☐ **main office**
- ☐ **principal**
- ☐ **secretary**
- ☐ **nurse's office**
- ☐ **nurse**
- ☐ **parking lot**
- ☐ **bus driver**

Find or draw more pictures of school places and workers. Add them to your Word File.

- ☐
- ☐ _____
- ☐
- ☐ _____

Vocabulary

School Places and Workers

👓 Look at each picture.

💬 Say who each person is. Say where each person is.

✍️ Then write the words that finish each sentence.

WORD BANK

librarian   principal

library   secretary

main office

1

librarian

The _____*librarian*_____

is in the _____*library*_____ .

2

The _____ and the

_____ are in the

_____ .

Vocabulary

School Places and Workers

Look at each picture.

Say who each person is. Say where each person is.

Then write the words that finish each sentence.

WORD BANK

bus driver   nurse
classroom   nurse's office
counselor   parking lot
counselor's office   teacher

3

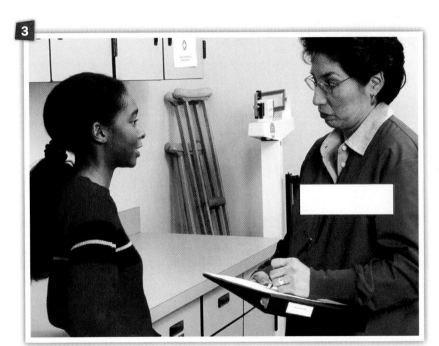

The _____

is in the _____ .

4

The _____

is in the _____ .

5

The _____

is in the _____ .

6

The _____

is in the _____ .

School Places and Workers

Look at each picture.

Say who each person is. Say where each person is.

Then write the words that finish each sentence.

WORD BANK

assistant principal	gym
auditorium	hallway
cafeteria	janitor
coach	students

7

The _____

are in the _____ .

8

The _____

is in the _____ .

9

The _____

is in the _____ .

10

The _____

is in the _____ .

Mr. Reyes is in the main office.

Use Words for School Places and Workers

Draw two places in your school. Write the name of each place. Write the people who work there. With a partner, look at your drawings. Say the name of each person. Say where each person is.

Listen and Say

Use a question like this to find out where a place is.

QUESTION	ANSWER
Where is _____ ?	Here it is.

> Where is the library?

> Here it is.

> Where is Room 115?

> Here it is.

Say It Another Way   CD 1 Track 29

When you ask where something is, use **where is** or **where's**.

Where is	Where's
Where is the library?	Where's the library?
Where is the cafeteria?	Where's the cafeteria?
Where is the gym?	Where's the gym?

Shorten the two words like this:

Add '

Where is = Where's

Take out a letter.

Say and Write

Ask a partner a question about a place on the map. Your partner points to the place and says "Here it is." Then write three questions.

Questions

1. Where is the _____ ?

2. Where is room _____ ?

3. _____ ____ the _____ ?

On Your Own

Draw a map of your school on a piece of paper.
Label places on your map.
Ask a partner about the places on your map.

Where is the cafeteria?

Ask and Answer Questions

Listen and Say

Use questions like these to ask about people.

QUESTIONS	ANSWERS
Who is the _____ ?	_____ is the _____ .
Who is _____ ?	_____ is the _____ .

1 "Who is the librarian?" "Mrs. López is the librarian."

2 "Who is Mr. Nguyen?" "Mr. Nguyen is the principal."

3 "Who is Ms. Thomas?" "Ms. Thomas is the counselor."

How It Works

A **question** asks for information. Start with the word that asks for what you want to know.

Question Word	Asks About
Who	a person
Where	a place
What	a thing
When	a time

Say and Write

✍️ Write words to finish each question. 🔄 Then give your book to a partner.
Answer your partner's questions. 💬 Say each question and answer.

Mrs. Martinez
Principal

Mrs. Hasan
Counselor

Mr. Carrido
Secretary

Mr. Koval
Janitor

4

Who is the ___secretary___ ?

___Mr. Carrido___ is the ___secretary___ .

5

Who _____ the counselor?

_____ is the

_____ .

6

_____ is _____ _____ ?

_____ _____ the

_____ .

7

Who is ___Mr. Koval___ ?

___Mr. Koval___ is the ___janitor___ .

8

Who _____ Mrs. Martinez?

_____ is the

_____ .

9

_____ is _____ ?

_____ _____ the

_____ .

On Your Own

🔄 Work with a partner. ✍️ Write the names
of people in your school or their roles on cards.
Use the cards to ask about people.

Who is Mrs.
Springer?

Mrs. Springer

Read and Retell

Build Background

Now you will read *Alexei's Week*. It is Alexei's first week at his new school.

Read

As you read, find out what happens to Alexei on each day of the week.

Collect Words

You know many words for school places and subjects. Write some of the words. Use the words to talk about the book.

Theme Book

CD 1 Track 31

Alexei's
Week
by Antonia Barber

Word Web

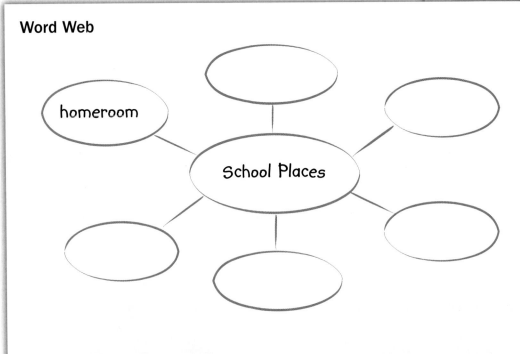

homeroom

School Places

Tell About the Book

1 Think about *Alexei's Week*. Write the name of each day. Then write what happens to Alexei on each day.

Day	Events
Monday	The bus is late. Alexei is lost.
Tuesday	

2 Use your chart to tell a partner about *Alexei's Week*.

Write About Your First Day in the U.S.A.

Study a Model

My First Day in the U.S.A., *by Marie Vincent*

Tuesday, 3:00 p.m.

I am in Miami.

Tuesday, 6:30 p.m.

I am at 349 Locust Street.
I meet Uncle Frank.

Focus on Capital Letters

Remember to start the names of cities with a **capital letter**. The names of streets also start with a capital letter.

I am in **M**iami.

> **capital letter**

I am at 349 **L**ocust **S**treet.

> **capital letters**

The names of people and days of the week start with a **capital letter**. Remember that **I** is always a capital letter.

I meet **U**ncle **F**rank on **T**uesday.

> **capital letters**

Write each word with a capital letter.

1 san francisco

_____

2 main street

_____

3 aunt natalya

_____

4 friday

_____

Write about your first day in the United States. Draw pictures or tape photos in the boxes. Tell where you are. Tell who you meet.

My First Day in the U.S.A.

by _____

Day: _____

Time: _____

Day: _____

Time: _____

Check Your Writing

Share your work with a partner. Check the writing. Did you use correct capital letters?

Unit 4

Everything You Do

Unit Project

Take photos of people in your class. Write something about each person or about groups of people.

In This Unit

Try Out Language	Vocabulary	Language Function	Patterns	Language Wrap-Up	Writing
Chant	Classroom Activities Words for People	Give Information	I am _____ . You are _____ .	**Language Game:** Act It Out!	Write About a Classmate
Chant	Outdoor Activities and Sports Words for People and Things	Give Information Ask and Answer Questions	He is _____ . She is _____ . It is _____ . Can you _____ ? Yes, I can. Can he _____ ? No, he cannot. Can she _____ ? No, she can't. Can it _____ ? Yes, it can.	**Theme Theater:** The Soccer Game	
Song	The Arts Words for People	Give Information Give Information	He is _____ . She is _____ . It is _____ . They are _____ . I can _____ . We can _____ . He can _____ . She can _____ . It can _____ . They can _____ .	**Read and Retell** Huong's Journey by Frank Hartley	

Theme Book

Listen and Chant

What Can You Do?

Open your book . Write your name.

Use a computer. Play a game.

Raise your hand . Work with a group.

Now what else can you do?

Make your own chant.

talk with a partner

read your book

close your book

listen to a CD

Word File

CLASSROOM ACTIVITIES
Check the words you know.

- [ ] take out your book
- [ ] open your book
- [ ] read your book
- [ ] close your book
- [ ] write your name
- [ ] listen to a CD
- [ ] raise your hand
- [ ] talk with a partner
- [ ] use a computer
- [ ] work with a group

91 _____ your book

92 _____ your book

93 _____ your book

94 _____ your book

95 _____ your name

96 _____ to a CD

97 _____ your hand

98 _____ with a partner

99 _____ a computer

100 _____ with a group

96 listen to a CD

97 raise your hand

98 talk with a partner

99 use a computer

100 work with a group

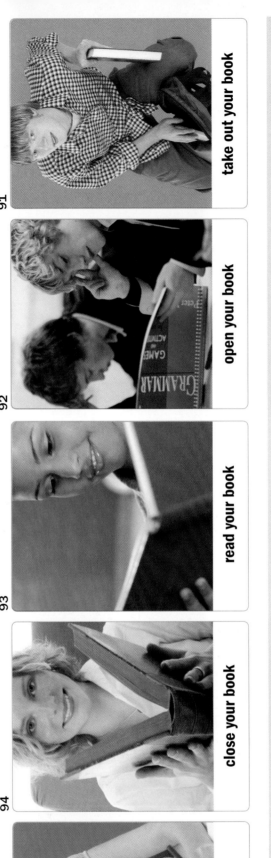

91 take out your book

92 open your book

93 read your book

94 close your book

95 write your name

Word File

CLASSROOM ACTIVITIES

Study and practice the words. Then check the words you use.

- [ ] **take out your book**
- [ ] **open your book**
- [ ] **read your book**
- [ ] **close your book**
- [ ] **write your name**
- [ ] **listen to a CD**
- [ ] **raise your hand**
- [ ] **talk with a partner**
- [ ] **use a computer**
- [ ] **work with a group**

Find or draw more pictures of other classroom activities. Add them to your Word File.

- [ ] _____
- [ ] _____
- [ ] _____
- [ ] _____
- [ ] _____
- [ ] _____

Words for People

When you talk about yourself, use **I**.

> **I** am Tomás.

When you talk with another person, use **you**.

> **You** are new at school. Are **you** from Mexico?

Look at each picture. Say the word that finishes each sentence.
Then write the word. Use *I* or *you*.

1

> _____I_____ am in math class.

3

> Are _____ in my gym class?

2

> _____ am from Haiti.

Use Words for People

Work with a partner.

Say things about each other.

Use the words

I and *you*.

> I am from Mexico. You are from China.

Vocabulary

Classroom Activities

 Look at each picture.

 Say the name of each activity.

 Then write the activity.

4. _____

5. _____

2. _____

1. open your book

3. _____

6. _____

7

8

9

10

Do Classroom Activities

Work with a partner. Say a classroom activity. Your partner will act out the activity.

Give Information

Listen and Say

Use sentences like these to talk about people.

| I am _____ . | You are _____ . |

1 I am a teacher.

2 I am in the library.

3 You are a student.

4 You are my partner.

How It Works

am	are
The verb **am** goes with **I**.	The verb **are** goes with **you**.
I am a student.	**You are** a bus driver.
I am from China.	**You are** in class.
I am at school.	**You are** from Korea.

Say and Write

Fill out the *I am* column. Work with a partner. Share your information with your partner. Then write your partner's information in the *You are* column.

	I am	You are
5 Tell your name.		
6 Tell where you are from.		
7 Tell what class you are in.		
8 Tell one more thing about yourself.		

On Your Own

Share your information with more people in your class.

I am Jae-Min.

Language Wrap-Up

Play a Game

How to Play

1. Play with a partner.

2. Use an eraser or other small object as your game piece.

3. Put your game piece on START.

4. Flip a coin to tell how many spaces to move.

 Heads = 1 space   Tails = 2 spaces

5. Read the sentence. Then do what it says.

Write your name.

6. Partners take turns.

7. The first player to reach FINISH wins.

Act It Out!

START

Take out your book.

Open your book.

Read your book.

Close your book.

Write your name.

Listen to a CD.

Raise your hand.

Talk with a partner.

Use a computer.

FINISH

Listen and Chant

That Sounds Like Fun!

Ride a skateboard

in the sun.

Swim in a pool.

That sounds like fun!

Make your own chant.

play soccer

throw a ball

walk in the park

run on a track

Word File

OUTDOOR ACTIVITIES AND SPORTS

Check the words you know.

- ☐ catch a ball
- ☐ kick a ball
- ☐ throw a ball
- ☐ play soccer
- ☐ ride a skateboard
- ☐ run on a track
- ☐ sit in a chair
- ☐ stand in line
- ☐ swim in a pool
- ☐ walk in the park

101
———— a ball

102
———— a ball

103
———— a ball

104
———— soccer

105
———— a skateboard

106
———— on a track

107
———— in a chair

108
———— in line

109
———— in a pool

110
———— in the park

106 run on a track

107 sit in a chair

108 stand in line

109 swim in a pool

110 walk in the park

101 catch a ball

102 kick a ball

103 throw a ball

104 play soccer

105 ride a skateboard

OUTDOOR ACTIVITIES AND SPORTS

Study and practice the words. Then check the words you use.

- ☐ catch a ball
- ☐ kick a ball
- ☐ throw a ball
- ☐ play soccer
- ☐ ride a skateboard
- ☐ run on a track
- ☐ sit in a chair
- ☐ stand in line
- ☐ swim in a pool
- ☐ walk in the park

Find or draw more pictures of outdoor activities or sports. Add them to your Word File.

- ☐ _____
- ☐ _____
- ☐ _____
- ☐ _____
- ☐ _____
- ☐ _____

Words for People and Things

Use **he** to talk about a man or a boy.

He is the coach.

Use **she** to talk about a woman or a girl.

She is the principal.

Use **it** to talk about an animal or a thing.

This is a flag.
It is on the flagpole.

Look at each picture. Say the word that finishes each sentence. Then write the word. Use *he*, *she*, or *it*.

1

_____He_____ is in the park.

3

_____ is a librarian.

4

_____ is on the field.

2

_____ is on the track.

Use Words for People

Work with a partner. Say a sentence about a person or thing in your school. Then your partner says the sentence with the word *he*, *she*, or *it*.

> Mr. Cruz is the coach.

> He is the coach.

Give Information

Listen and Say

Use sentences like these to talk about one other person or thing.

| He is _____ . | She is _____ . | It is _____ . |

1

He is a bus driver.
He is in the parking lot.

2

She is a coach.
She is in the gym.

3

Here is a ball.
It is brown.

How It Works

Use **is** with **he**, **she**, and **it**.

he	she	it
He **is** from Vietnam. He **is** a counselor.	She **is** a secretary. She **is** in the main office.	This **is** a notebook. It **is** blue.

© NGSP & HB

Say and Write

 Look at each picture. Say the words that finish each sentence. Then write the words.

4

____She____ ____is____ a
bus driver.

5

That is a ball.

_____ _____ on

the water.

6

_____ _____ in
the cafeteria.

7

_____ _____
from South Korea.

8

That is a computer. _____

_____ on the steps.

9

_____ _____ in the gym.

On Your Own

Work with a partner. Use your picture
cards from Unit 3. Tell who each school
worker is. Then tell where each worker is.

He is the assistant principal.
He is in the hallway.

Ask and Answer Questions

Listen and Say

People and animals can do many things. Use sentences like these to talk about things they can do.

QUESTIONS	ANSWERS		
Can you _____ ?	Yes, **I** can.	No, **I** cannot.	No, **I** can't.
Can Andy _____ ?	Yes, **he** can.	No, **he** cannot.	No, **he** can't.
Can Lin _____ ?	Yes, **she** can.	No, **she** cannot.	No, **she** can't.
Can a dog _____ ?	Yes, **it** can.	No, **it** cannot.	No, **it** can't.

Can You Swim?

Marc: Hi, Inez. My family is going to the lake on Saturday.

Inez: That sounds fun! Can you swim?

Marc: Yes, I can.

Inez: Can your sister swim?

Marc: No, she can't swim. She is too young.

Inez: Can the dog swim?

Marc: Yes, it can. It can swim well.

Say It Another Way

Use **cannot** or **can't** to talk about things you cannot do.

cannot	can't
I cannot throw a *ball*. She cannot swim.	I can't throw a *ball*. She can't swim.

Shorten **cannot** like this:

I cannot = I can't

© NGSP & HB

Say and Write

Look at each picture. Say the words that finish each question and answer. Then write the words.

1

_____Can_____ John swim?

_____Yes_____, _____he_____ _____can_____ .

2

Can you __throw__ a ball?

_____Yes_____, _____I_____ _____ .

3

_____ Mike ride a skateboard?

_____No_____, _____ _____ .

4

_____ the dog catch the ball?

_____, _____ _____ .

On Your Own

Work with a partner. Ask your partner two questions with *can*. Your partner answers the questions. Then join another pair of students. Ask about each other and answer the questions.

Can Joe catch a baseball?

Yes, he can.

Theme Theater

Juana, Brian, and Diego are at a soccer game. They are watching their friend Laura play soccer. Listen to their conversation. Then act it out.

THE SOCCER GAME

JUANA: Where is Laura? Can you see her?

BRIAN: She is on the field.

DIEGO: I see her!

JUANA: Look at her kick the soccer ball! She scored a goal!

[The crowd cheers.]

CHORUS: *Laura kicked the soccer ball.*
She scored a goal.

◊   ◊   ◊

CHORUS **BRIAN** **DIEGO** **JUANA**

DIEGO: Brian, can you play soccer?

BRIAN: Yes, I can. It is fun!

DIEGO: Juana, can you play soccer?

JUANA: No, I can't. But I can ride a skateboard. That is more fun. Diego, can you ride a skateboard?

DIEGO: Yes, I can. I can play soccer, too.

CHORUS: *Brian can play soccer.*
Diego can play soccer, too.
Juana can't play soccer.
She can ride a skateboard.

◊   ◊   ◊

BRIAN: I am hungry. I want a hot dog.

JUANA: You are always hungry!

DIEGO: You can stand in line. You can buy a hot dog.

JUANA: Then you can eat.

DIEGO: Wait! Laura kicked the ball again.

JUANA: It's another goal!

[The crowd cheers.]

CHORUS: *Laura can kick the ball!*
And Brian can eat!

CD 2 Track 8
Tune: "You're A Grand Old Flag"

Things We Can Do

I can sing a song.
He can act in a play.
These are things we can do every day!

We can play the drums.
It's really fun!
We do many things every day.

I can paint and draw.
She can play the guitar.
These are things we can do every day!

We all can do so many things.
We want you to join us today!

Word File

THE ARTS
Check the words
you know.

- ☐ act in a play
- ☐ dance to the music
- ☐ draw a picture
- ☐ paint a picture
- ☐ play the drums
- ☐ play the guitar
- ☐ play the piano
- ☐ sing a song
- ☐ take a picture
- ☐ write a story

111

_____ in a play

116

_____ the guitar

112

_____ to the music

117

_____ the piano

113

_____ a picture

118

_____ a song

114

_____ a picture

119

_____ a picture

115

_____ the drums

120

_____ a story

116 play the guitar

111 act in a play

117 play the piano

112 dance to the music

118 sing a song

113 draw a picture

119 take a picture

114 paint a picture

120 write a story

115 play the drums

Word File

THE ARTS
Study and practice the words. Then check the words you use.

- [ ] **act in a play**
- [ ] **dance to the music**
- [ ] **draw a picture**
- [ ] **paint a picture**
- [ ] **play the drums**
- [ ] **play the guitar**
- [ ] **play the piano**
- [ ] **sing a song**
- [ ] **take a picture**
- [ ] **write a story**

Find or draw more pictures of the arts. Add them to your Word File.

- [ ] _____
- [ ] _____
- [ ] _____
- [ ] _____
- [ ] _____
- [ ] _____

Vocabulary

Words for People

When you talk about yourself and another person, use **we.**

We are in a play.

When you talk about other people, use **they.**

They are in a play.

👓 Look at each picture. 💬 Say the word that finishes each sentence.

✍ Then write the word.

1

___They___ are in the band.

4

_____ are in the picture.

2

_____ are actors.

5

_____ are in the choir.

3

_____ are musicians.

Use Words for People

💬 Work with a group. Talk about yourselves and other people in your classroom. Use the words *we* and *they.*

Give Information

Listen and Say

Use these words to talk about people, animals, and things.

| He is _____ . | She is _____ . | It is _____ . | They are _____ . |

1 He is a soccer player.

3 It is a piano.

5 They are red.

2 She is a janitor.

4 They are in the gym.

6 They are pets.

How It Works

One Person or Thing	Sometimes you talk about only one other person or thing. Use the verb **is**.	He **is** in science class. She **is** in the auditorium. It **is** green.
More Than One Person or Thing	Other times, you talk about more than one person or thing. Use the verb **are**.	They **are** in science class. They **are** in the auditorium. They **are** green.

Say and Write

Look at each picture. Say the words that finish each sentence. Then write the words.

7 ___They___ ___are___ on the bench.

10 _____ _____ the coach.

8 _____ _____ a soccer player.

11 _____ _____ on the field.

9 _____ _____ at the game.

12 Where is the ball? _____ _____ on the field.

On Your Own

Work with a partner. Look around your classroom or school. Talk about the people and things you see. Use *he*, *she*, *it* and *they*.

They are brown.

135

Give Information

Listen and Say

Use words like these when you tell what people and things can do.

ONE	MORE THAN ONE		ONE	MORE THAN ONE
I can _____ .	We can _____ .		He can _____ . She can _____ . It can _____ .	They can _____ .

The Talent Show

Charlie: Hey, Vidas and Ann. There is a school talent show next month. Do you want to play in it?

Ann: Yes. We can play a song together.

Charlie: I can play the drums.

Vidas: I can play the piano.

Ann: We need a guitar player.

Vidas: I have a friend. He can play the guitar.

Ann: All our friends will watch. They can dance to the music.

Charlie: It will be fun!

How It Works

If you are not sure when to use **he, she, it,** or **they**, ask yourself these questions:

Are you talking about ...	Then use ...
one man or boy?	he
one woman or girl?	she
one thing?	it
more than one other person or thing?	they

Say and Write

Look at each picture. Say the words that finish the sentence.
Then write the words.

1

___I___ ___can___ play the piano.

2

___They___ _____ sing.

3

_____ _____ play the guitar.

4

_____ _____ play the drums.

5

_____ _____ write a story.

6

_____ _____ take a picture.

On Your Own

Draw pictures of yourself and your friends or family. Write three things that each person can do.

Work with a partner. Talk about the things you can do. Talk about the things other people can do.

Carmen is my sister. She can sing.

Language Wrap-Up

Read and Retell

Build Background

Now you will read *Huong's Journey*. Huong is an artist from Vietnam.

Read

As you read, find out about Huong's life and what she likes to paint.

Collect Words

You know many words for the arts. Write some of the words. Write any new words you learned. Use the words to talk about the book.

Theme Book

CD 2 Track 11

Huong's Journey
by Frank Hartley

Word Web

paint

The Arts

Retell the Story in Sequence

1 Think about Huong's life. What happened first? Write it in the first box.

Huong lived in Vietnam.

2 Now write three more events in the other boxes.

3 Use your chart to tell a partner about Huong's life.

Writing

Write About a Classmate

Study a Model

Can you play the drums?

Yes, I can.

An Interview with Boris Lubov

Martina: What is your name?

Boris: My name is Boris.

Martina: Where are you from?

Boris: I am from Russia.

Martina: Where do you live?

Boris: I live at 15 Oak Street.

Martina: Can you play the guitar?

Boris: No, I can't.

Martina: Can you play the drums?

Boris: Yes, I can. I can play well.

Martina: Thank you, Boris.

Boris: You're welcome.

Focus on Sentences

Use a **question mark** at the end of a question.

Can you play the guitar? ← question mark

Remember to start every sentence with a **capital letter**. Put a **period** at the end of every statement.

capital letter
Can you sing?
Yes, I can. ← period
capital letter

Write each sentence correctly.

1 what is your name

_____

2 my name is kim

_____

3 can you play the drums

_____

4 no, i can't

_____

140

© NGSP & HB

Draw a picture of a classmate you will interview.
Write four questions. Ask the classmate your questions.
Then write the answers.

An Interview with _____

Q. _____

A. _____

Q. _____

A. _____

Q. _____

A. _____

Q. _____

A. _____

Check Your Writing

Share your work with a partner. Check the writing. Do you need to add a question mark to the end of a question? Do you start each sentence with a capital letter? Do you end each answer with a period?

Unit 5   At Lunch

Unit Project

Bring food from home. Show the class how to make your favorite food.

In This Unit

Try Out Language	Vocabulary	Language Function	Patterns	Language Wrap-Up	Writing
Chant	Food Food Counts	Give Information	*This is _____ .* *That is _____ .* *These are _____ .* *Those are _____ .*	Language Game: Name That Food!	Write About Your Favorite Food
Chant	Food	Express Likes and Dislikes	*Do you like _____ ?* *Yes, I like _____ .* *No, I do not like _____ .* *I don't like _____ .*	Theme Theater: Pizza or Pasta?	
Song	Money	Buy and Sell	*How much is _____ ?* *The _____ is _____ .* *How much are _____ ?* *The _____ are _____ .* *How much does it cost?* *It costs _____ .* *How much do they cost?* *They cost _____ .*	Read and Retell	

Lunch Around the World

BY LOUISE FRANKLIN

Theme Book

Listen and Chant

Buy some rice for a tasty treat.

Red chili rice is good to eat!

Buy some bread for a tasty treat.

Pita bread is good to eat!

Make your own chant.

beans

cheese

corn

© NGSP & HB

Word File

FOOD
Check the words you know.

- ☐ **apple**
- ☐ **banana**
- ☐ **orange**
- ☐ **beans**
- ☐ **bread**
- ☐ **cheese**
- ☐ **corn**
- ☐ **lettuce**
- ☐ **milk**
- ☐ **onion**
- ☐ **rice**
- ☐ **tomato**

121

122

123

124

125

126

127

128

129

130

126 lettuce

127 milk

128 onion

129 rice

130 tomato

121 orange apple banana

122 beans

123 bread

124 cheese

125 corn

Word File

FOOD

Study and practice the words. Then check the words you use.

- ☐ **apple**
- ☐ **banana**
- ☐ **orange**
- ☐ **beans**
- ☐ **bread**
- ☐ **cheese**
- ☐ **corn**
- ☐ **lettuce**
- ☐ **milk**
- ☐ **onion**
- ☐ **rice**
- ☐ **tomato**

Find or draw more pictures of foods. Add them to your Word File.

- ☐ _____
- ☐ _____
- ☐ _____
- ☐ _____
- ☐ _____
- ☐ _____

© NGSP & HB

Vocabulary

Food Counts

one	more than one

Use numbers or words like **some** to describe more than one thing.
Often, you add **-s** to the name, too.

one apple ⟶ three apple**s**   one onion ⟶ some onion**s**

Add -s.

💬 Say the name of each picture.   ✍ Write the word. Add -s for more than one.

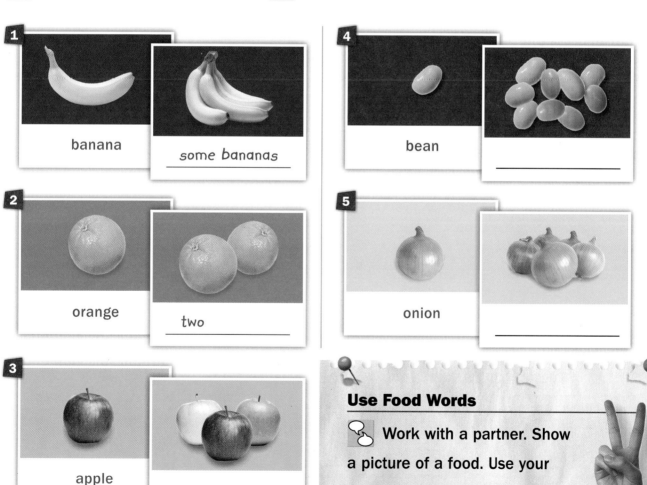

1 banana — *some bananas*

2 orange — *two* _____

3 apple — _____

4 bean — _____

5 onion — _____

Use Food Words

💬 Work with a partner. Show a picture of a food. Use your fingers to show how many. Say the number and the food.

Vocabulary

Food

Look at each picture.

Say the name of each food.

Then write the name.

WORD BANK

apple	lettuce
banana	milk
beans	onion
bread	orange
cheese	rice
corn	tomato

1. milk
2.
3.
4.
5.
6.
7.
8.

9

10

11

12

Use Food Words

👐 You and a partner are shopping. Tell your partner what to buy.

	two	
	three	
Buy	some	_____ .
	a	
	an	
	the	

Listen and Say

Use these words to point out things.

This is _____ .	That is _____ .	These are _____ .	Those are _____ .

1 What is this?   This is a tomato.

3 What are these?   These are tomatoes.

2 What is that?   That is a tomato.

4 What are those?   Those are tomatoes.

How It Works

	Close to You	Far From You
One Thing	What is this? This is _____ .	What is that? That is _____ .
More Than One Thing	What are these? These are _____ .	What are those? Those are _____ .

Say and Write

  Look at each picture. Say the words that finish each sentence.
Then write the words.

5

What is this?

__This__ __is__ a bean.

6

What are those?

_____ __are__ bananas.

7

What are these?

_____ _____ apples.

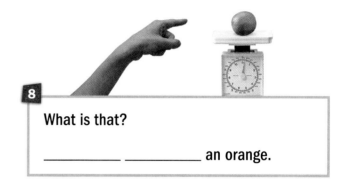

8

What is that?

_____ _____ an orange.

9

What are those?

_____ _____ _____ .

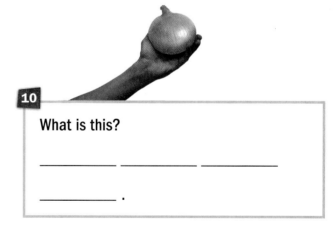

10

What is this?

_____ _____ _____

_____ .

On Your Own

 Work with a partner. Talk about foods you see in the cafeteria.

These are apples.

Language Wrap-Up

Play a Game

How to Play

1. Work with a partner. Draw foods on your game board. Write their names.

2. Partner 1 tosses a coin onto the game board to make it land on a food. Then Partner 1 asks a question about the food.

   > What are these?

3. Partner 2 answers.

   > Those are bananas.

4. Partner 2 tosses the coin to ask about another food.

5. Partners take turns.

6. Find a new partner. Play again.

Name That Food!

bananas

Try Out Language

CD 2 Track 14

Listen and Chant

Foods I Like!

I like tacos.

I like cheese.

I like bok choy,

But I don't like peas!

tacos

cheese

bok choy

peas

Make your own chant.

carrots

soup

pizza

pasta

peppers

sushi

154   Unit 5 | At Lunch

© NGSP & HB

FOOD

Check the words
you know.

- ☐ chicken
- ☐ chips
- ☐ salsa
- ☐ egg
- ☐ hamburger
- ☐ hot dog
- ☐ pizza
- ☐ salad
- ☐ sandwich
- ☐ soup
- ☐ taco

131

132

133

134

135

136

137

138

139

140

136 pizza

131 chicken

137 salad

132 chips salsa

138 sandwich

133 egg

139 soup

134 hamburger

140 taco

135 hot dog

Word File

FOOD

Study and practice the words. Then check the words you use.

- ☐ chicken
- ☐ chips
- ☐ salsa
- ☐ egg
- ☐ hamburger
- ☐ hot dog
- ☐ pizza
- ☐ salad
- ☐ sandwich
- ☐ soup
- ☐ taco

Find or draw more pictures of foods. Add them to your Word File.

- ☐ _____
- ☐ _____
- ☐ _____
- ☐ _____
- ☐ _____
- ☐ _____

Food

💬 Say the name of each food. ✎ Then write the name.

1

soup

sandwich

2

3

4

5

6

7

Use Food Words

💬 Ask a partner, "What's for lunch?"
Point to the food your partner names.
Use words like these.

What's for	breakfast lunch dinner	?

Express Likes and Dislikes

Listen and Say

Use sentences like these to talk about what you like and do not like.

QUESTION	ANSWERS		
Do you like _____ ?	Yes, I like _____ .	No, I do not like _____ .	I don't like _____ .

The Hot Dog Stand

Mr. Jones: Do you like hot dogs?

Mrs. Lee: I don't know.

Marisa: Yes, I like hot dogs.

Mr. Lee: No, I do not like hot dogs. I don't like them at all!

Mr. Jones: But my hot dogs are great! Please have one.

Mrs. Lee: Yum! It's good. I like your hot dogs.

Say It Another Way   CD 2 Track 16

People use many words to describe food or feelings.

	😠	😐	🙂	😋
Food	Yuck! It is awful!	So-so. It is not good.	Ok. It is good.	Yum! It's great!
Feelings	I hate it!	I don't like it.	I like it.	I love it!

Say and Write

 Look at each picture. Do you like this food?

Write *I like* or *I don't like* to complete each sentence.

1

_____ I like _____ pizza.

2

_____ carrots.

3

_____ chicken.

4

_____ cheese.

5

_____ salad.

6

_____ tacos.

On Your Own

Work with a partner. Use your pictures.

Tell about foods you like and don't like.

I do not like hamburgers.

Theme Theater

Lydia and Marcos are buying lunch at the cafeteria.
But Marcos can't decide what to eat. Listen to their
conversation. Then act it out.

PIZZA OR PASTA?

[The lunch bell rings.]

LYDIA: Pizza or pasta? I know what I want!

MARCOS: Pizza or pasta? Hmm …

LYDIA: Oh no! Not again, Marcos!

MARCOS: What?

LYDIA: You can never choose what to eat for lunch.
We spend our whole lunchtime in line!

◊   ◊   ◊

WORKER: What can I get for you?

LYDIA: Pizza, please.

WORKER: Here you go.

◊   ◊   ◊

WORKER: What would you like?

MARCOS: Hmm …

LYDIA: Oh no! Here we go!

CHORUS: *Pizza or pasta? What will he choose?*
Can we get some pizza or pasta for you?

CHORUS   **WORKER**   **MARCOS**   **LYDIA**

WORKER: Do you know what you want?

MARCOS: Lydia, what should I get?

LYDIA: Marcos, just choose the pizza. Then we can get our food and sit down.

◈   ◈   ◈

WORKER: Well?

MARCOS: I agree with Lydia. I'll have pizza today.

WORKER: Do you want cheese pizza or pepperoni pizza?

MARCOS: Cheese or pepperoni? Hmm. What should I choose?

LYDIA: Oh no! Not again.

[The lunch bell rings.]

CHORUS: *Cheese or pepperoni? He can't decide.*
Now lunchtime is over, and they're still in line!

CD 2 Track 18

Tune: "Oh! Susanna"

Listen and Sing

How Much Is It ?

How much does this pasta cost?
How much is that rice?
How much does a hot dog cost?
I need to know the price.

The pasta costs four dollars.
The rice costs even more.
A hot dog is $2.50,
but it's cheaper than before.

© NGSP & HB

Word File

MONEY
Check the words
you know.

- [ ] **bills**
- [ ] **one dollar**
- [ ] **five dollars**
- [ ] **ten dollars**
- [ ] **twenty dollars**
- [ ] **coins**
- [ ] **penny**
- [ ] **nickel**
- [ ] **dime**
- [ ] **quarter**

141

142

143

144

145

146

147

148

149

150

146 coins

147 penny   A penny is one cent.

148 nickel   A nickel is five cents.

149 dime   A dime is ten cents.

150 quarter   A quarter is twenty-five cents.

141 bills

142 one dollar

143 five dollars

144 ten dollars

145 twenty dollars

Word File

MONEY

Study and practice the words. Then check the words you use.

- ☐ **bills**
- ☐ **one dollar**
- ☐ **five dollars**
- ☐ **ten dollars**
- ☐ **twenty dollars**
- ☐ **coins**
- ☐ **penny**
- ☐ **nickel**
- ☐ **dime**
- ☐ **quarter**

Find or draw more pictures of money. Add them to your Word File.

- ☐ _____
- ☐ _____
- ☐ _____

Vocabulary

Money

wallet

Write what is in the wallet.

1

This is a _____one dollar bill_____ .

2

This is ____ten____ cents.

3

This is a _____ .

4

This is a _____ .

5

This is _____ cents.

6

This is _____ cents.

7

This is _____ dollars.

Use Money Words

Work with a partner.

Point out bills and coins.

These are coins.

Buy and Sell

Listen and Say

Use sentences like these when you buy or sell things.

How much is _____ ?	How much are _____ ?	How much does it cost?	How much do they cost?
The _____ is _____ .	The _____ are _____ .	It costs _____ .	They cost _____ .

1 "How much is the hamburger?" "The hamburger is $1.80."

2 "How much does it cost?" "The pizza costs $16.27."

3 "How much are those fries? How much do your drinks cost?" "The fries are 95¢. Our drinks cost 65¢ each."

Say It Another Way

	✏️ **Write It**	💬 **Say It**
	dollar sign $1.27 **decimal point**	"A dollar and twenty-seven cents" "One twenty-seven" "A buck twenty-seven"
	cent symbol 65¢ $0.65	"Sixty-five cents"

Say and Write

  Look at each picture. Say the words that finish each question and answer. Then write the words.

4

How much _are these eggs_ ?

The eggs _are_ $4.75.

5

How much _do these_

cost? The tacos _are_

$1.20 each.

6

How much _____

cost? The bagels _____

95¢ each.

7

How much _____ ?

The banana _____ 40¢.

8

How much _____ ?

The salad _____ $5.00.

9

How much do _____

cost? Two hot dogs _____

$4.50.

On Your Own

Show your partner a picture. Your partner asks how much the food costs. Decide on a price and answer your partner.

The apple is $0.85.

Language Wrap-Up

Read and Retell

Build Background

Now you will read *Lunch Around the World*. Lunch is the meal that many people eat at noon.

Read

As you read, find out what people around the world eat for lunch.

Collect Words

You know many words for food and money. What new words did you learn in this book? Write the words. Use the words to talk about the book.

Theme Book

CD 2 Track 21

Lunch Around the World

BY LOUISE FRANKLIN

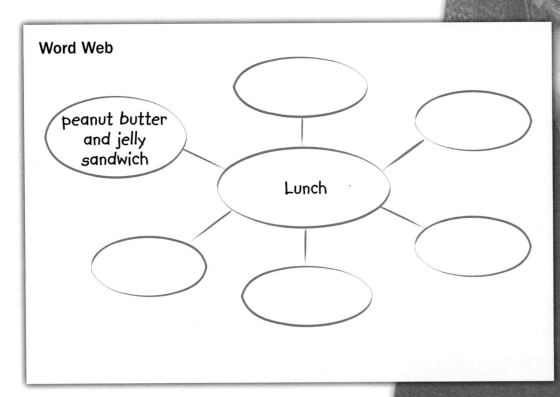

Word Web

peanut butter and jelly sandwich

Lunch

Tell About the Book

1 Think about the book. What is it mainly about? Write a sentence in the box.

> People eat different things for lunch.

2 Think about details that tell about this main idea. Add them to the diagram.

> People eat different things for lunch.

Mateo likes empanadas for lunch.

3 Make a new diagram.

> People like to eat many of the same foods.

Many people like to eat burgers.

4 Use your diagrams to tell a partner about *Lunch Around the World*.

Write About Your Favorite Food

Chalupas

I like chalupas because they are crunchy and spicy.
To make chalupas, you need:

6 tortillas
1 cup of cheese
1 can of black beans
1 tomato
1 onion
3 chile peppers
1 avocado
lettuce

Focus on Plurals

You can count some foods, like peppers and onions. When you name more than one, add -**s**.

1 chile pepper

3 chile pepper**s**

✐ Write the plural form of each word.

1 🍌 _____
banana

2 🍎 _____
apple

3 🍊 _____
orange

✍ Write about your favorite food. Draw a picture or tape a photo of it to this page.

_____

I like _____ because _____

_____

To make _____ , you need:

_____

_____

_____

_____

_____

_____

_____

_____

_____

_____

Check Your Writing

👥 Share your work with a partner. Check the writing. Do you need to add -s to make a word plural?

Unit 6

Information Everywhere

Unit Project

Make a book with
your classmates.
Include photos
and labels.

In This Unit

Try Out Language	Vocabulary	Language Function	Patterns	Language Wrap-Up	Writing
Chant	Print Materials Parts of a Book	Express Needs and Wants	*I need a _____ .* *I need some _____ .* *I want a _____ .* *I want some _____ .*	**Language Game:** I Want _____ . I Need _____ .	Write How to Do Something
Song	Technology Computer Words	Give and Follow Commands	*call* *give* *listen* *make* *play* *print* *take* *turn on / turn off* *write*	**Theme Theater:** The School Dance	
Chant	Signs and Safety Location Words	Give Commands	*Be careful!* *Go that way!* *Help!* *Hurry up!* *Slow down!* *Stop!* *Watch out!*	**Read and Retell**	

The *Race Around* the **World**
by Lili Henderson

Theme Book

Listen and Chant

I Need Some Information

I need a newspaper.
I need a magazine.
I need some information
About something I have seen.

I need a dictionary.
I need a textbook.
I need the meaning of a word.
Please show me where to look.

© NGSP & HB

Word File

PRINT MATERIALS
Check the words you know.

- [ ] advertisement
- [ ] bulletin board
- [ ] announcement
- [ ] dictionary
- [ ] encyclopedia
- [ ] envelope
- [ ] letter
- [ ] stamp
- [ ] magazine
- [ ] newspaper
- [ ] poster
- [ ] sign
- [ ] textbook

151

152

153

154

155

156

157

158

159

160

magazine

156

newspaper

157

poster

158

sign

WEBSTER GROVES HIGH SCHOOL
HOME OF THE STATESMEN

159

textbook

160

advertisement

151

announcement

Student Council Meeting
Friday at 4:00 p.m.
School Cafeteria

bulletin board

152

dictionary

153

encyclopedia

154

stamp
envelope
letter

155

Word File

PRINT MATERIALS

Study and practice the words. Then check the words you use.

- [ ] **advertisement**
- [ ] **bulletin board**
- [ ] **announcement**
- [ ] **dictionary**
- [ ] **encyclopedia**
- [ ] **envelope**
- [ ] **letter**
- [ ] **stamp**
- [ ] **magazine**
- [ ] **newspaper**
- [ ] **poster**
- [ ] **sign**
- [ ] **textbook**

Find or draw more pictures of print materials. Add them to your Word File.

- [ ] _____
- [ ] _____
- [ ] _____
- [ ] _____
- [ ] _____
- [ ] _____

Parts of a Book

Look for these parts at the front of a book.

cover   title page   table of contents

 Look at the parts of the book. Read each question.
Then write the answer for each question.

1 What is the title?

_____

2 Who is the author?

_____

3 Who is the publisher?

_____

4 What is the title of Chapter 2?

_____

5 On which page does Chapter 3 start?

_____

6 How many chapters are there?

_____

Talk About Books

Take out a book. With a partner, compare your books. Talk about the title, author, publisher, and the table of contents for each book.

© NGSP & HB

Vocabulary

Print Materials

 Look at each picture.

 Say the name of each item.

 Then write the name.

WORD BANK

advertisement	encyclopedia	poster
announcement	envelope	publisher
author	letter	sign
bulletin board	magazine	stamp
chapter title	newspaper	textbook
dictionary	page number	title

THE COMPLETE INTERNET GUIDE for Students

MYRA CHAVEZ

1 author

THE COMPLETE INTERNET GUIDE for Students

MYRA CHAVEZ

WATSON PUBLISHERS

2

3

NONFICTION

talk

WEEKLY

Save up to 65%

SALE

GEO

the ZONE

VIRTUAL world

4

5

6

7

8

CONTENTS

CHAPTER 1
Searching the Internet ...8

CHAPTER 2
Using the Internet
for Research 18

CHAPTER 3
Creating Your Own
Web Page..............38

CH
Staying Safe
on the Internet 60

9

14

16

Book Club
will meet
on Thursday

READ

10

15

11

17

18

12

Tt

13

A B C D E F G H I J K

ENCYCLOPEDIA

Talk About Print Materials

Bring an example of a print material to class. Make a class collection. Compare print materials with a partner.

Express Needs and Wants

Listen and Say

Use sentences like these to tell what you need or want.

I need a _____ .	I need some _____ .	I want a _____ .	I want some _____ .

1 I need a dictionary.

3 I want a book about sports.

2 I need some stamps.

4 I want some magazines about dogs.

Use the Right Word

a, an	some
Use **a** or **an** to talk about one thing that is not specific.	Use **some** to talk about more than one thing.
I need **a** stamp.	I need **some** stamps.
I need **an** envelope.	I need **some** envelopes.
I want **a** magazine.	I want **some** magazines.

Say and Write

 Look at each picture. Say the words that finish the sentence.
Then write the words.

5

I __want__ a book about sports.

7

_____ some magazines.

9

I need _____ _____ .

6

_____ encyclopedia.

8

_____ _____ envelopes.

10

_____ _____ _____ _____ .

On Your Own

Work with a partner. Use your pictures.
Choose a card. Tell your partner what you want
or need from the card. Use *a, an,* or *some.*
Take turns until you use all the cards.

I need a magazine.

Play a Game

How to Play

1. Play with a partner.

 1   **2**

2. Each partner chooses a mark. X O

3. Partner 1 chooses a square and says a sentence.

    I need some stamps.

4. If the sentence is correct, Partner 1 draws his or her mark in the square.

5. Partners take turns.

6. Get three marks in a row to win.

I Want _____.

I Need _____.

Technology Is Good

Technology is good.
It helps us keep in touch.
So call me on your cell phone.
We can talk about so much.

Computers help us find
A lot of facts for school.
They help us write things faster.
Don't you think they're really cool?

Word File

TECHNOLOGY
Check the words you know.

- ☐ camera
- ☐ cell phone
- ☐ computer
- ☐ copier
- ☐ DVD player
- ☐ laptop computer
- ☐ music player
- ☐ speakers
- ☐ television
- ☐ video camera

161

162

163

164

165

166

167

168

169

170

laptop computer

166

music player

167

speakers

168

television

169

video camera

170

camera

161

cell phone

162

computer

163

copier

164

DVD player

165

Word File

TECHNOLOGY

Study and practice the words. Then check the words you use.

- ☐ **camera**
- ☐ **cell phone**
- ☐ **computer**
- ☐ **copier**
- ☐ **DVD player**
- ☐ **laptop computer**
- ☐ **music player**
- ☐ **speakers**
- ☐ **television**
- ☐ **video camera**

Find or draw more pictures of technology. Add them to your Word File.

- ☐ _____
- ☐ _____
- ☐ _____
- ☐ _____
- ☐ _____
- ☐ _____

Computer Words

- CD and DVD drive
- icon
- printer
- screen
- computer
- monitor
- disk drive
- CD or DVD
- shift
- delete
- enter
- space
- mouse
- keyboard

Use Computer Words

Work with a partner. Find a computer in your classroom or school. Name the parts of the computer.

© NGSP & HB

Vocabulary

Technology

👓 Look at each picture. Read each sentence.

💬 Say the name of each type of technology.

✍ Then write the name.

1

You can use the Internet on a
laptop computer .

2

You can call someone on a
_____ .

3

You can make a video with a
_____ .

4 You can print out information
with a _____ .

6 You can type on a
_____ .

5 You can find information
with a _____ .

10 You can watch videos on a _____ .

11 You can play videos with a _____ .

7 You can take a picture with a _____ .

8 You can listen to music with a _____ .

9 You can make copies with a _____ .

Use Technology Words

Work with a partner. Talk about something you can do with each type of technology.

I can _____ with a _____ .

Give and Follow Commands

Listen and Say

When you want someone to do something, use a command.
Many commands start with these words.

call	give	listen	make	play	print	take	turn on	turn off	write

Watching a Video

Mr. Buzad: We are going to watch a video today. Listen carefully and take notes, please. Arun, please play the video.

Arun: The DVD player doesn't work.

Mr. Buzad: Turn on the DVD player.

Arun: Oh, yes.

Mr. Buzad: Thank you, Arun. Students, write your names on your papers. Please give me your notes at the end of class.

Use the Right Word

Some verbs have two words. Many two-word verbs use the word **turn**.
Look at the second word to find the meaning.

turn on	turn off	turn up	turn down
Use **on** with **turn** to talk about making something start.	Use **off** with **turn** to talk about making something stop.	Use **up** with **turn** to talk about making something louder.	Use **down** with **turn** to talk about making something quieter.
Turn **on** the television.	Turn **off** the printer.	Turn **up** the music.	Turn **down** the music.

© NGSP & HB

Say and Write

Look at each picture. Say the command that finishes the sentence. Then write the command.

1. ___Call___ your friend.

2. _____ three copies.

3. _____ a picture.

4. _____ to music.

5. _____ a DVD.

6. _____ _____ the monitor.

On Your Own

Work with a partner. Use your pictures. Say what you do with each thing. Give a command. Your partner acts out the command.

Turn off the television.

Theme Theater

Vanna and Gustavo are planning the school dance.
Listen to their conversation. Then act it out.

THE SCHOOL DANCE

GUSTAVO: We need some signs for the dance.

VANNA: Here's a sign. I made it on my computer.

GUSTAVO: OK. Turn on the copier.
We can make some copies.

VANNA: We can put the signs on the bulletin
boards in the hallways.

GUSTAVO: That plan is great! Please make some copies.

CHORUS: *Vanna and Gustavo need some signs for the dance.*

◇   ◇   ◇

MR. LOUIS: I like the sign. When is the dance?

GUSTAVO: It is next Friday.

MR. LOUIS: Hmm. March 10 is tomorrow.

VANNA: Oh, no! I got the wrong date!

CHORUS: *The sign is great.*
But Vanna got the wrong date.

◇   ◇   ◇

CHORUS   **MR. LOUIS**   **GUSTAVO**   **VANNA**

VANNA: I need a computer to make a new sign.
I can use the computer in the library.

MR. LOUIS: Call the librarian on my cell phone.
Ask her to meet you there.
She can help you.

VANNA: Thank you, Mr. Louis.
Gustavo, please take down
these signs. I will make new signs.

◇　　◇　　◇

*[It is the day of the dance. Vanna and
Gustavo are in the gym.]*

GUSTAVO: We are ready for the dance.
The CDs and speakers
are in the gym.

VANNA: Yes, everything is ready!
We need a camera.
I want pictures of the dance.

GUSTAVO: I have a camera.
I can take pictures.

VANNA: Great! Call me later.
Meet me before the dance.

GUSTAVO: See you later!

CHORUS: *Everything is ready!*
They are ready for the dance!

Look at the Signs

Stop! Watch out!

Don't cross the street.

Now the light is red.

You must wait to move your feet.

Look at the signs.

They're important, you know.

They tell you when to stop.

They tell you when to go.

Word File

SIGNS AND SAFETY
Check the words you know.

- ☐ bathroom sign
- ☐ bus stop sign
- ☐ crossing sign
- ☐ crossing light
- ☐ exit sign
- ☐ hospital sign
- ☐ railroad crossing sign
- ☐ speed limit sign
- ☐ stop sign
- ☐ traffic light

171

Here is the boys' bathroom.

172

A bus stops here. You can get on or off the bus.

173

People can cross the street here.

174

The signal tells when it is safe to cross.

175

Go this way to get outside.

176

A hospital is near.

174

Cars cross the railroad tracks here.

171

Cars stop here.

175

Slow down! A school is near.

172

The light tells cars when to stop and go.

176

173

Word File

SIGNS AND SAFETY
Study and practice the words. Then check the words you use. Draw two more signs on the blank cards.

- [ ] **bathroom sign**
- [ ] **bus stop sign**
- [ ] **crossing sign**
- [ ] **crossing light**
- [ ] **exit sign**
- [ ] **hospital sign**
- [ ] **railroad crossing sign**
- [ ] **speed limit sign**
- [ ] **stop sign**
- [ ] **traffic light**

Find or draw more pictures of signs for information and safety. Add them to your Word File.

- [ ] _____
- [ ] _____
- [ ] _____
- [ ] _____
- [ ] _____
- [ ] _____

Vocabulary

Location Words

Some words help you know where something is.

The stop sign is **at** the corner.

The exit sign is **on** the wall.

The speed limit sign is **next to** the street.

 Look at each picture. Say the words that finish each sentence. Then write the words.

1

The _bathroom_ sign is _on_ the door.

3

The _____ _____ is _____ _____ the street.

2

The _____ _____ sign is _____ the corner.

Use Location Words

Work with a partner. Look for signs around your school. Tell your partner where each sign is.

Give Commands

Listen and Say

Use these urgent commands to get someone to act fast.

Be careful!	Go that way!	Help!	Hurry up!	Slow down!	Stop!	Watch out!

1 Go that way!
Hurry up!

2 Stop!
Watch out!

3 Slow down!
Be careful!

4 Help!

How It Works

There are different ways to ask or tell a person what to do. Use polite commands when there is no emergency. Use urgent commands when you need to act fast.

Polite Commands	Urgent Commands
Use the word **please** at the beginning or the end.	Make them short. Use your voice to show strong feeling.
Polite commands end with a **period** (.).	An urgent command ends with an **exclamation point** (!).
Please listen to the CD. Listen to the CD, **please.**	Stop! Slow down!

© NGSP & HB

Say and Write

Look at the signs. Say the name of each sign.

Draw a picture of a sign in each box. Then write an urgent command on each line.

5

_____

6

_____

7

_____

8

_____

On Your Own

Work with a partner.
Act out each command.

Stop!

Language Wrap-Up

Read and Retell

Build Background

Now you will read *The Race Around the World*. You will travel to different places on a race around the world.

Read

As you read, find out how clues and signs help you in the race.

Collect Words

You know many words for different kinds of places. Write some of these words. Write any new words you learn. Use the words to talk about the book.

Theme Book

CD 2 Track 29

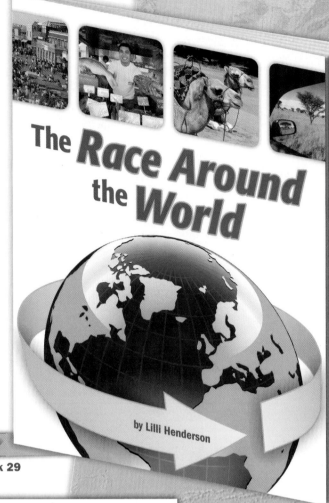

The **Race Around** the **World**

by Lilli Henderson

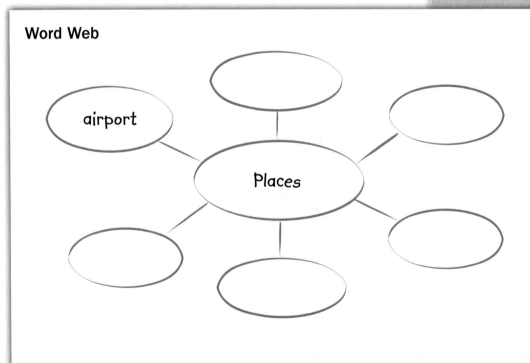

Word Web

airport

Places

Tell About the Book

1 Think about where you find clues in the race. Write the name of each city and country in the chart.

2 Think about the clues you find in each city. Add them to the chart.

City, Country	Clues
Los Angeles, United States	1. Fly to Mexico City. Find Duarte's flower shop on Vicente Guerrero Street.
Mexico City, Mexico	

3 Use your chart to tell a partner about *The Race Around the World.*

Write How to Do Something

Study a Model

How to Send an E-mail

1. Open your e-mail program.
2. Click **New** to write a new e-mail.
3. In the **To** box, type the e-mail address of the person you want to write to.
4. In the **Subject** box, type the subject of the e-mail.
5. In the **message window**, type your message.
6. Don't forget to click **Send** to send your e-mail!

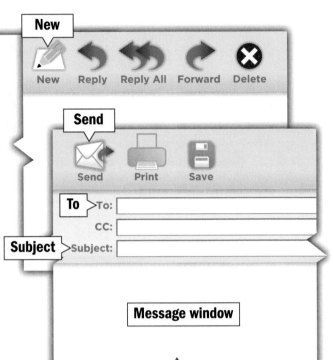

Focus on Sentences

A **statement** tells you something. It ends with a **period**.

I want to send an e-mail.< **period**

A **command** tells someone to do something. Many commands end with a **period**.

Open your e-mail program.< **period**

A command that shows strong feeling ends with an **exclamation point**.

Don't forget to click Send to send your e-mail!< **exclamation point**

Remember that all statements and commands begin with a capital letter.

Write each sentence correctly.

1 watch out

_____

2 please give me your phone number

_____

3 i need to send an e-mail

_____

4 slow down

_____

Write steps for how to do something. Draw a picture.
Label the picture.

How to _____

1. _____

   _____

2. _____

   _____

3. _____

   _____

4. _____

   _____

5. _____

   _____

6. _____

   _____

Check Your Writing

 Share your work with a partner. Check the writing.

Did you start each sentence with a capital letter? Did you

use periods and exclamation points correctly?

Unit 7

How Do You Feel?

Unit Project

Create a video or post photos on a Web page to show how people feel.

In This Unit

Try Out Language	Vocabulary	Language Function	Patterns	Language Wrap-Up	Writing
Chant	Parts of the Body Describing Words	Describe Yourself Describe Other People	I am _____ . I have _____ _____ . My _____ is _____ . My _____ are _____ . He is _____ . She has _____ _____ . His _____ is _____ . Her _____ are _____ .	Language Game: Draw a Face	Describe a Friend
Chant	Parts of the Body Health Words	Express Feelings	How do you feel? I feel fine. I feel bad. My _____ hurts. I have a _____ .	Theme Theater: At the Doctor's Office	
Song	Feelings	Express Feelings	How do you feel? I am _____ . I feel _____ .	Read and Retell	

How Do They Feel?

by Frank Hartley

Theme Book

Listen and Chant

CD 3 Track 1

Parts of Your Body

Touch your [head].

Point to your cheek.

Close your eyes.

Now listen to me.

Touch your [nose].

Point to your chin.

Open your eyes.

Now do it again.

Make your own chant. Act it out.

ear

face

lips

neck

hair

© NGSP & HB

Word File

PARTS OF THE BODY
Check the words you know.

- ☐ cheek
- ☐ chin
- ☐ ear
- ☐ eye
- ☐ face
- ☐ hair
- ☐ head
- ☐ mouth
- ☐ lip
- ☐ tooth
- ☐ neck
- ☐ throat
- ☐ nose

177

178

179

180

181

182

183

184

185

186

182 hair

183 head

184 tooth lip mouth

185 throat neck

186 nose

177 cheek

178 chin

179 ear

180 eye

181 face

Word File

PARTS OF THE BODY

Study and practice the words. Then check the words you use.

- [ ] **cheek**
- [ ] **chin**
- [ ] **ear**
- [ ] **eye**
- [ ] **face**
- [ ] **hair**
- [ ] **head**
- [ ] **mouth**
- [ ] **lip**
- [ ] **tooth**
- [ ] **neck**
- [ ] **throat**
- [ ] **nose**

Find or draw more pictures of parts of the body. Add them to your Word File.

- [ ] _____
- [ ] _____
- [ ] _____
- [ ] _____
- [ ] _____
- [ ] _____

Describing Words

Some describing words tell what a person looks like.

brown hair

long hair

a young woman

tall   short

short hair

blue eyes

an old man

Look at each picture. Say the words that finish each sentence. Then write the words.

1

He is _____ a _____ young _____ man.

He has _____ red _____ hair.

2

She is _____ _____ woman.

She has _____ _____ .

3

He is _____ _____ _____ .

He is _____ .

Use Describing Words

Work with a partner. Use your pictures. Talk about the people. Use describing words.

She is a young woman.

182

Describe Yourself

Listen and Say

Use sentences like these to tell what you look like.

I am _____ .	I have _____ _____ .	My _____ is _____ . My _____ are _____ .

What Do You Look Like?

Uncle Tonio: Hello, Pedro. I am coming to visit you soon!

Pedro: I am happy! I will see you at the airport.

Uncle Tonio: Tell me what you look like now.

Pedro: Well, I am tall. My hair is brown. And I have brown eyes. What do you look like?

Uncle Tonio: I am tall, too. I have gray hair. And my eyes are blue.

Pedro: OK. See you soon, Uncle Tonio! Have a safe trip!

How It Works

Use **I** to talk about yourself.

Use **my** to tell about something you own.

I ⟶ my

I	I am young. I am tall.
my	My eyes are brown. My hair is short. My hair is black.

Look at the picture. Say the words that finish each sentence.
Then write the words.

3 I have _____ _____.

1 My _____eyes_____ _____are_____ _____brown_____.

5 _____ _____ tall.

2 I am _____.

4 I _____ _____ _____.

6 My _____ _____ _____.

On Your Own

 Work with a partner. Tell your partner what
you look like. Then tell another partner.

I have brown hair.
My eyes are brown.

Describe Other People

Listen and Say

Use sentences like these to tell what other people look like.

| He is _____ . | He has _____ _____ . | His _____ is _____ . | His _____ are _____ . |
| She is _____ . | She has _____ _____ . | Her _____ is _____ . | Her _____ are _____ . |

Waiting for Friends

Pilar: Hi, Michael. What are you doing?

Michael: I am waiting for my friends, Paulo and Stacey. We are going to see a movie.

Pilar: Oh. What does Paulo look like?

Michael: He is tall. He has short hair. His eyes are brown.

Pilar: OK. What does Stacey look like?

Michael: She is short. She has black hair. Her hair is long.

Pilar: Oh, I see them. Here they come now!

How It Works

he → his
she → her

Use **he** to talk about a man or a boy. Use **his** to talk about something he owns.

Use **she** to talk about a woman or a girl. Use **her** to talk about something she owns.

Man or boy	he	He is old.
	his	His eyes are brown.
Woman or girl	she	She is young.
	her	Her eyes are green.

Say and Write

 Look at each picture. Say the words that finish each sentence.

 Then write the words.

1

____He____ ____is____ tall.

3

_____ has long hair.

5

_____ eyes _____ brown.

2

_____ _____ young.

4

_____ _____

_____ hair.

6

_____ _____ _____

blond.

On Your Own

 Work with a partner. Find pictures of people in magazines

or a newspaper. Tell your partner what each person looks like.

 Write the sentences that your partner uses on the lines below.

_____

_____

_____

_____

Describe Other People **213**

Language Wrap-Up

Play a Game

How to Play

1. Play with a partner.

2. Use two coins as markers.

3. Partner 1 tosses a coin onto Board 1. Then Partner 1 tosses another coin onto Board 2. Partner 1 uses the two words in a sentence.

Her hair is brown.   She has a little nose.

4. Then Partner 1 draws the body part.

5. Partner 2 takes a turn.

6. A person who lands on a body part that he or she has already drawn loses a turn.

7. The first person to draw a complete face wins. The winner describes the face.

She has green eyes.
Her hair is brown.

Draw a FACE

Parts of the Body

Board 1	cheeks	chin	ears	eyes
	hair	head	mouth	neck	nose

Describing Words

Board 2	big	little	short	long
	blue	black	brown	green	red

Listen and Chant

HOW DO **YOU** FEEL?

How do you feel?

I feel bad.
My head hurts,
And it makes me sad!

How do you feel?

I feel bad.
My arm hurts,
And it makes me sad!

Make your own chant.

stomach

hand

back

leg

© NGSP & HB

PARTS OF THE BODY

Check the words you know.

- ☐ **arm**
- ☐ **elbow**
- ☐ **back**
- ☐ **body**
- ☐ **chest**
- ☐ **foot**
- ☐ **ankle**
- ☐ **toe**
- ☐ **hand**
- ☐ **finger**
- ☐ **thumb**
- ☐ **wrist**
- ☐ **hip**
- ☐ **leg**
- ☐ **knee**
- ☐ **shoulder**
- ☐ **stomach**

187

188

189

190

191

192

193

194

195

196

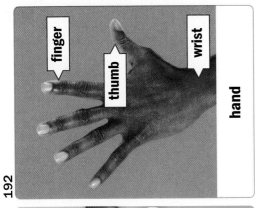

192   finger   thumb   wrist   hand

193   hip

194   knee   leg

195   shoulder

196   stomach

187   elbow   arm

188   back

189   body

190   chest

191   ankle   toe   foot

Word File

PARTS OF THE BODY

Study and practice the words. Then check the words you use.

- ☐ arm
- ☐ elbow
- ☐ back
- ☐ body
- ☐ chest
- ☐ foot
- ☐ ankle
- ☐ toe
- ☐ hand
- ☐ finger
- ☐ thumb
- ☐ wrist
- ☐ hip
- ☐ leg
- ☐ knee
- ☐ shoulder
- ☐ stomach

Find or draw more pictures of parts of the body. Add them to your Word File.

- ☐ _____
- ☐ _____
- ☐ _____
- ☐ _____
- ☐ _____
- ☐ _____

Health Words

Sometimes you feel bad because you have:

a headache

a toothache

a fever

an earache

a stomachache

a cold

 Read each sentence. Say the words that finish each sentence.

 Then write the words.

1 My head is hot.

I have a ___fever___ .

2 My stomach hurts.

I have a _____ .

3 My tooth hurts.

I have _____ _____ .

4 My ear hurts.

I have _____ _____ .

5 My nose hurts.

I have _____ _____ .

6 My head hurts.

I have _____ _____ .

Use Health Words

Work with a partner. Read the sentences on this page. Act out how you feel.

© NGSP & HB

Vocabulary

Parts of the Body

Look at each picture.

Say the name of each body part.

Then write the name.

WORD BANK

ankle	hip
arm	knee
back	leg
body	shoulder
chest	stomach
elbow	thumb
finger	toe
foot	wrist
hand	

1 arm

2

3

4

5

6

7

8

9

10

Express Feelings

CD 3 Track 5

Listen and Say

Use sentences like these to tell how you feel.

QUESTION	ANSWERS			
How do you feel?	I feel fine.	I feel bad.	My _____ hurts.	I have a _____ .

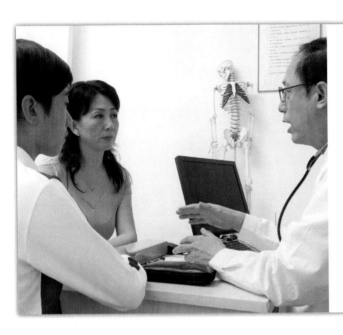

The Doctor's Office

Doctor: How do you feel, Mrs. Cheng?

Mrs. Cheng: I feel fine. But my son Lee feels bad.

Doctor: How do you feel, Lee?

Lee: I feel bad. My ear hurts. I have an earache.

Doctor: I can help you. Come with me. I need to look in your ear.

Say It Another Way

CD 3 Track 6

There are many ways to say how you feel.

When You Feel Good	When You Feel Bad
I feel good. I feel fine. I'm OK. I feel great!	I feel bad. I don't feel well. I'm sick. I feel terrible!

Say and Write

 Look at each picture. Say the words that finish each question and answer.

Then write the words.

1 How do you feel?

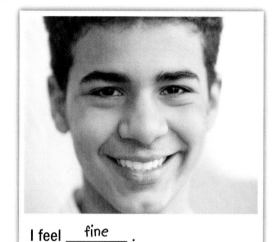

I feel ___fine___ .

2 How do _____ _____ ?

I feel _____ .

My _____ hurts.

3 How _____ _____ _____ ?

I _____ _____ .

I have a _____ .

4 _____ _____ _____ feel?

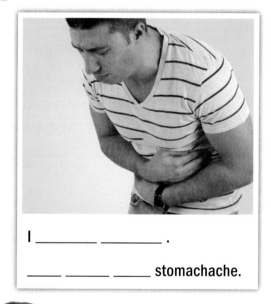

I _____ _____ .

_____ _____ _____ stomachache.

On Your Own

 Work with a partner. Use your pictures.
Choose a picture card. Ask your partner,
"How do you feel?" Your partner answers.

How do you feel?

I feel bad.
My back hurts.

Theme Theater

Juanita is at the doctor's office with her mother. Listen to their conversation. Then act it out.

AT THE DOCTOR'S OFFICE

DR. SMITH: Hello, Juanita. Hello, Mrs. Campos.

MRS. CAMPOS: Hello, Dr. Smith.

JUANITA: Hi, Dr. Smith.

DR. SMITH: You look sick, Juanita. How do you feel?

JUANITA: I feel bad.

◊   ◊   ◊

DR. SMITH: I'm sorry to hear that. Tell me more.

JUANITA: My ear hurts. I feel terrible!

MRS. CAMPOS: She has a fever.

CHORUS: *Juanita feels terrible!*
She has a fever.

CHORUS   MRS. CAMPOS   JUANITA   DR. SMITH

JUANITA: I want to feel better, Dr. Smith. I want to play soccer on Saturday.

MRS. CAMPOS: She needs some medicine.

DR. SMITH: I will give you medicine. It will help your earache and fever.

JUANITA: Can I play soccer on Saturday?

DR. SMITH: Yes, you can. Go home and rest. Drink lots of water. Take the medicine. You will feel better soon.

CHORUS: *Juanita will feel better soon. She can play soccer on Saturday.*

◊   ◊   ◊

MRS. CAMPOS: Thank you, Dr. Smith.

DR. SMITH: You're welcome. Have a nice day.

JUANITA: Good-bye, Dr. Smith.

CHORUS: *Juanita will feel better soon. They say "good-bye" and "thank you."*

Listen and Sing

HOW I FEEL

You ask how I feel.
I feel confused.
I feel proud.
How about you?

You ask how I feel.
I feel sad.
I feel happy.
I feel glad.

Make your own song.

surprised

scared

angry

© NGSP & HB

Word File

FEELINGS

Check the words you know. Draw two more faces with other feelings on the blank cards.

- ☐ **angry**
- ☐ **bored**
- ☐ **confused**
- ☐ **happy**
- ☐ **proud**
- ☐ **sad**
- ☐ **scared**
- ☐ **surprised**

197

198

199

200

201

202

203

204

205

206

202 **proud**

203 **sad**

204 **scared**

205 **surprised**

206

197 **angry**

198 **bored**

199 **confused**

200 **happy**

201

Word File

FEELINGS

Study and practice the words. Then check the words you use.

- ☐ **angry**
- ☐ **bored**
- ☐ **confused**
- ☐ **happy**
- ☐ **proud**
- ☐ **sad**
- ☐ **scared**
- ☐ **surprised**

Find or draw more pictures of feelings. Add them to your Word File.

- ☐ _____
- ☐ _____
- ☐ _____
- ☐ _____
- ☐ _____
- ☐ _____

Vocabulary

Feelings

 Look at each picture. Say the word that finishes each sentence. Then write the word.

1

I am _____scared_____ .

4

I am _____ .

6

I am _____ .

2

I am _____ .

5

I am _____ .

7

I am _____ .

3

I am _____ .

Use Words for Feelings

Work with a partner. Write the feelings on cards. Choose a card. Act out the feeling. Then your partner guesses the feeling.

surprised

Express Feelings

CD 3 Track 9

Listen and Say

Use sentences like these to tell how you feel.

QUESTION	ANSWERS	
How do you feel?	I am _____ .	I feel _____ .

First Place

Clara: How do you feel?

Isabel: I feel happy. Our team won the game! We got first place!

Clara: I am proud.

Isabel: I am surprised. I did not think we would win.

Clara: But we have a great team!

Say It Another Way   CD 3 Track 10

People use different words to describe the same feeling.

Feeling	happy	sad	scared	angry
Other Words	glad pleased	unhappy	afraid frightened	mad upset

© NGSP & HB

Say and Write

 Look at each picture. Say the words that finish each question and answer.
Then write the words.

1 How do you feel?

I feel __proud__ .

2 How do you _____ ?

I feel _____ .

3 How do _____ _____ ?

_____ am _____ .

4 How _____ _____ feel?

I feel _____ .

5 How _____ _____ _____ ?

I _____ _____ .

6 _____ _____ _____ _____ ?

_____ _____ _____ .

On Your Own

Work with a partner. Ask, "How do you feel?" Your partner answers and acts out the feeling.

How do you feel?

I am happy.

Language Wrap-Up

Read and Retell

Build Background

Now you will read *How Do They Feel?* It is about how different people feel in different situations.

Read

As you read, find out how people feel and why they feel this way.

Collect Words

You know many words for feelings. What new words did you learn in this book? Write the words. Use the words to talk about the book.

Theme Book

CD 3 Track 11

How Do They Feel?

by Frank Hartley

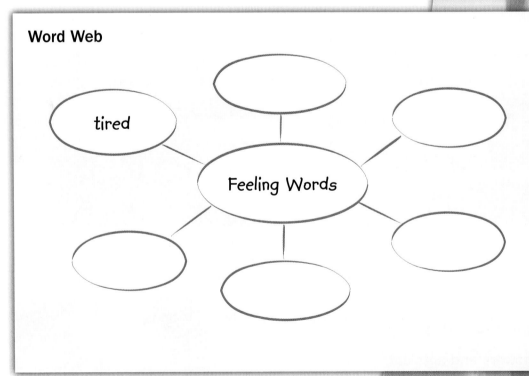

Word Web

tired

Feeling Words

Tell About the Book

1 Think about the people in *How Do They Feel?* Write the name of each person.

Name	Feeling	Why?
Taiki	tired	He studies karate. He practices too much.

2 Think about how each person feels. Write one feeling for each person.

3 Then think about why each person feels that way. Finish the chart.

4 Use your chart to tell a partner how each person feels and why.

Describe a Friend

Study a Model

Maria has green eyes.

Her hair is red.
She has long hair.

This is Maria!

Focus on Words for People

Use **he** and **his** when talking about a man or a boy. Use **she** and **her** when talking about a woman or a girl.

| he his | Chen has brown eyes. **He** has short hair. **His** hair is black. |

| she her | Celia has green eyes. **She** has brown hair. **Her** hair is long. |

 Write the word that finishes each sentence.

1 Juan has short hair.

_____ has brown eyes.

2 Sarah has blue eyes.

_____ hair is red.

3 Victor has blonde hair.

_____ eyes are green.

4 Carina has brown eyes.

_____ has long hair.

Describe a friend. Finish each sentence below.

Then write your own sentences. Draw pictures of your friend.

Fold here.

_____ has _____ eyes.   _____ hair is _____ .

_____ has _____ hair.

This is _____ !

Check Your Writing

Share your work with a partner. Check the writing.

Did you use *he* or *his* to describe a man or a boy? Did you

use *she* or *her* to describe a woman or a girl?

Unit 8

Brrr! Put On Your Coat!

Unit Project

Design a T-shirt, jeans, or hat that shows your history and personality.

In This Unit

Try Out Language	Vocabulary	Language Function	Patterns	Language Wrap-Up	Writing
Song	Clothing Time Order Words	Ask and Answer Questions	*Does the _____ have _____ ?* *Yes, it does.* *No, it does not.* *No, it doesn't.* *Do the _____ have _____ ?* *Yes, they do.* *No, they do not.* *No, they don't.*	Language Game: I'm Ready!	Write a Letter and a List
Chant	Clothing Describing Words	Describe Things Ask and Answer Questions	*Here is a _____ .* *It has _____ .* *Here are some _____ .* *They have _____ .* *Which _____ do you like?* *I like this / that / these / those _____ .*	Theme Theater: Sneakers for Silvia	
Chant	Weather Describing Words	Express Ideas	*It's _____ today.* *I need to _____ .* *I want to _____ .* *I have to _____ .*	Read and Retell **What Should I Wear?** by Frank Hartley	

Theme Book

Listen and Sing

The Clothing MACHINE

Socks and shoes,
Jackets and jeans,
Shirts and skirts,
I'm a clothing machine!

Make your own song.

pants

belts

dresses

sweaters

© NGSP & HB

CLOTHING

Check the words you know.

- ☐ belt
- ☐ buckle
- ☐ dress
- ☐ jacket
- ☐ collar
- ☐ zipper
- ☐ jeans
- ☐ pants
- ☐ shirt
- ☐ pocket
- ☐ shoes
- ☐ skirt
- ☐ socks
- ☐ sweater
- ☐ button

207

208

209

210

211

212

213

214

215

216

212

shirt

pocket

213

shoes

214

skirt

215

socks

216

sweater

button

207

belt

buckle

208

dress

209

jacket

collar

zipper

210

jeans

211

pants

Word File

CLOTHING

Study and practice the words. Then check the words you use.

- ☐ **belt**
- ☐ **buckle**
- ☐ **dress**
- ☐ **jacket**
- ☐ **collar**
- ☐ **zipper**
- ☐ **jeans**
- ☐ **pants**
- ☐ **shirt**
- ☐ **pocket**
- ☐ **shoes**
- ☐ **skirt**
- ☐ **socks**
- ☐ **sweater**
- ☐ **button**

Find or draw more pictures of clothing. Add them to your Word File.

- ☐ _____
- ☐ _____
- ☐ _____
- ☐ _____
- ☐ _____
- ☐ _____

Vocabulary

Time Order Words

Use these words to put actions in order.

First, I put on my shirt.

Next, I put on my jeans.

Then, I put on my socks.

Last, I put on my shoes.

👀 Look at each picture. 💬 Say the words that finish each sentence. ✍ Then write the words.

1

First, I put on my

____shirt____ .

_____ , I put on my

_____ .

_____ , I put on my

_____ .

_____ , I put on my

_____ .

✍ Write about what you put on first, next, then, and last.

2 _____ , I put on my _____ .

_____ , I put on my _____ .

_____ , I put on my _____ .

_____ , I put on my _____ .

Use Time Order Words

💬 Work with a partner. Tell what you put on in time order.

© NGSP & HB

Vocabulary

Clothing

👓 Look at the pictures.

💬 Say the name of each piece of clothing.

✍ Then write the name.

1. dress
2.
3.
4.
5.

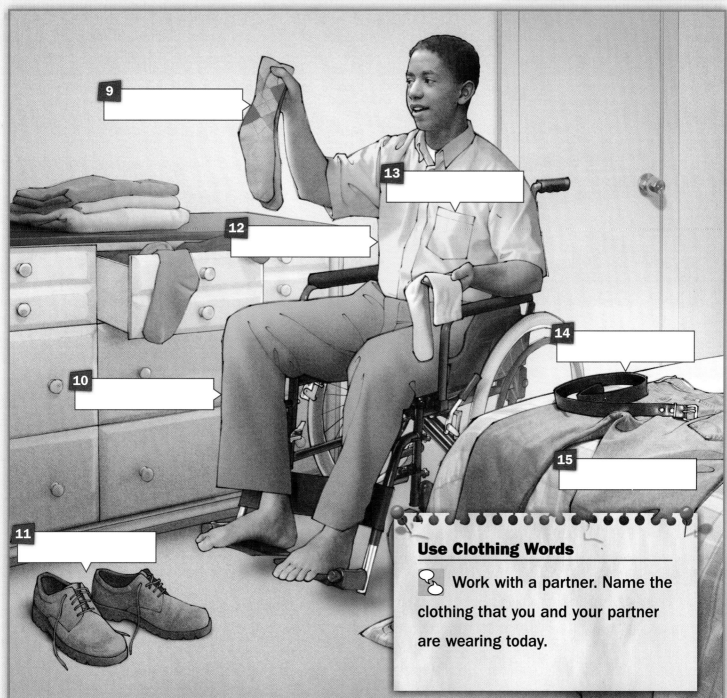

Ask and Answer Questions

Listen and Say

Use questions like these to find out information.

QUESTIONS	ANSWERS		
Does the _____ have _____ ? Do the _____ have _____ ?	Yes, it does. Yes, they do.	No, it does not. No, they do not.	No, it doesn't. No, they don't.

A Shirt and Shoes for Uncle Guillermo

Domingo: Here's the shirt for Uncle Guillermo.

Mom: Does the shirt have a collar?

Domingo: Yes, it does. He likes shirts with collars.

Mom: OK. Does the shirt have a pocket?

Domingo: No, it doesn't. Now look at these shoes.

Mom: Do the shoes have buckles?

Domingo: No, they don't. Here, look at them.

Mom: Oh, yes. Uncle Guillermo will like them!

Say It Another Way

 CD 3 Track 14

	does not / do not	doesn't / don't
When you talk about one thing, use **does not** or **doesn't**. ┌─────────────┐ ┌──────────┐ │ Take out a letter. │ │ Add an ' │ └─────────────┘ └──────────┘ does nø̸t = doesn't	The shirt **does not** have a pocket. The sweater **does not** have buttons.	The shirt **doesn't** have a pocket. The sweater **doesn't** have buttons.
When you talk about more than one thing, use **do not** or **don't**. ┌─────────────┐ ┌──────────┐ │ Take out a letter. │ │ Add an ' │ └─────────────┘ └──────────┘ do nø̸t = don't	The shirts **do not** have pockets. The sweaters **do not** have zippers.	The shirts **don't** have pockets. The sweaters **don't** have zippers.

Say and Write

 Look at each picture. Say the words that finish each question and answer. Then write the words.

1

Does the _shirt_ _have_ a collar?

Yes, it does .

2

_____ the _____ _____ a pocket?

_____ .

3

_____ the _____ _____ buttons?

_____ .

4

_Do_ the _skirts_ _have_ pockets?

No, they do not .

5

_____ the _____ _____ zippers?

_____ .

6

_____ the _____ _____ collars?

_____ .

On Your Own

 Work with a partner. Look at pictures of clothing in magazines. Take turns asking and answering questions about the clothing.

Does the shirt have a collar?

Yes, it does.

Language Wrap-Up

Play a Game

How to Play

1. Draw a different piece of clothing in each square on the game board.

2. Use coins as markers.

3. Your teacher says the name of a piece of clothing.

> Shirt

4. If the clothing is on your game board, put a marker on the square.

5. When you have three markers in a row, call out, "I'm ready!"

6. Other students ask questions about the clothing in your row.

> Does the shirt have a collar?

7. If you answer the questions correctly, you win. If not, take away the markers and keep playing.

I'm Ready!

READY TO GO!

Zip up those cool boots.

Put on your brown jacket.

Get your hat.

Grab your gloves.

Tie your scarf.

Get all snug.

Time to go to school.

© NGSP & HB

Word File

CLOTHING
Check the words you know.

- ☐ **boots**
- ☐ **heel**
- ☐ **coat**
- ☐ **sleeve**
- ☐ **gloves**
- ☐ **hat**
- ☐ **mittens**
- ☐ **sandals**
- ☐ **strap**
- ☐ **scarf**
- ☐ **shorts**
- ☐ **stripe**
- ☐ **sneakers**
- ☐ **shoelace**
- ☐ **T-shirt**

217

218

219

220

221

222

223

224

225

226

strap

222 sandals

heel

217 boots

sleeve

coat

218 coat

scarf

223 scarf

gloves

219 gloves

stripe

224 shorts

hat

220 hat

shoelace

225 sneakers

mittens

221 mittens

T-shirt

226 T-shirt

CLOTHING

Study and practice the words. Then check the words you use.

- ☐ **boots**
- ☐ **heel**
- ☐ **coat**
- ☐ **sleeve**
- ☐ **gloves**
- ☐ **hat**
- ☐ **mittens**
- ☐ **sandals**
- ☐ **strap**
- ☐ **scarf**
- ☐ **shorts**
- ☐ **stripe**
- ☐ **sneakers**
- ☐ **shoelace**
- ☐ **T-shirt**

Find or draw more pictures of clothing. Add them to your Word File.

- ☐ _____
- ☐ _____
- ☐ _____
- ☐ _____
- ☐ _____
- ☐ _____

Describing Words

Describing words can tell what something looks like or how it feels.

Colors and Sizes	Textures		Kinds

a small, yellow T-shirt

soft mittens

smooth boots

a shirt with long sleeves

a wool scarf

 Look at each picture. Say the words that finish each sentence. Then write the words.

1

This is a __large__, __blue__ sweater.

2

I need a shirt with _____ sleeves.

3

I want some _____ boots with a _____ heel.

Use Describing Words

Work with a partner. Look at pictures of clothing in a magazine. Use describing words to talk about the clothing.

Describe Things

Listen and Say

Use sentences like these to name something and tell what it is like.

Here is a _____ . It has _____ .	Here are some _____ . They have _____ .

1

Here is a shirt.
It has short sleeves.

2

Here are some sneakers.
They have red stripes.

How It Works

When you describe one thing, use has.
The *boot* **has** a high heel.
The *shirt* **has** white stripes.

When you describe more than one thing, use have.
The *boots* **have** high heels.
The *shirts* **have** short sleeves.

When you describe jeans, pants, and shorts, use have.
The *jeans* **have** two pockets.
The *pants* **have** a zipper.
The *shorts* **have** blue stripes.

Say and Write

Look at each picture. Say the words that finish each sentence. Then write the words.

3

Here is a __belt__ .

It has __a__ __big__ __buckle__ .

4

Here is __a__ __T-shirt__ .

It _____ _____ sleeves.

5

Here _____ _____ _____ .

It _____ _____ _____ .

6

Here are some _____ .

They have _____ _____ .

7

Here are _____ _____ .

They _____ _____ _____ .

8

Here _____ _____ _____ .

_____ _____ _____ .

On Your Own

Draw a game board of nine spaces. Then draw a picture of clothing in each space. Use different colors. Choose a mark: X or O. Describe the clothing in a space. Then draw your mark on the space. Take turns with a partner. Get three Xs or Os in a row to win.

Ask and Answer Questions

CD 3 Track 17

Listen and Say

Use sentences like these to tell which thing you like.

QUESTION	ANSWERS	
Which _____ do you like?	I like this _____ . I like that _____ .	I like these _____ . I like those _____ .

Shopping for Clothes

Rebecca: I like these shirts. Which shirt do you like, Jen?

Jen: I like that shirt. Gina, which shirt do you like?

Gina: I like this shirt. It is blue.

Jen: They are both nice.

Rebecca: Which shirt will you buy?

Jen: I will buy the blue one. I need a blue shirt.

Use the Right Word

You can use the words **which** and **what** to ask questions.

which	what
Use **which** when you ask about specific things. **Which** color do you like?	Use **what** when you are **not** asking about a specific thing. **What** color do you like?

The shirts are two different colors. I wonder which color you like.

I wonder what color you like best.

Say and Write

Look at each picture. Say the words that complete each question and answer. Then write the words.

1

Which __shirt__ do you like?

I like __this__ shirt.

3

_____ _____ do you like?

_____ _____ _____ belt.

2

Which __pants__ do you like?

I like _____ pants.

4

_____ jeans _____

_____ _____ ?

_____ _____ jeans.

On Your Own

Work with a partner. Look in a clothing catalog. Talk about the clothing. Ask your partner which clothing he or she likes. Your partner points to the clothing and answers the question.

Which shoes do you like?

I like those shoes.

Language Wrap-Up

Theme Theater

Fernando and Myra are shopping for a gift for Silvia.
Silvia is Fernando's sister. Listen to their conversation.
Then act it out.

SNEAKERS FOR SILVIA

FERNANDO: It's my sister Silvia's birthday. What can I buy?

MYRA: What does she want?

CHORUS: *What does Silvia want?*

FERNANDO: She wants some sneakers.

MYRA: Great! Here are the shoes for women.

SALESPERSON: May I help you?

FERNANDO: I want some sneakers for my sister. She likes red.

CHORUS: *Silvia likes red. She wants some sneakers.*

◇   ◇   ◇

SALESPERSON: Here are some sneakers. They have red shoelaces.

FERNANDO: I like those shoes.

MYRA:	Look! Here are some red boots. I like these boots.
FERNANDO:	Silvia wants sneakers. What else do you see?
SALESPERSON:	Here are some sneakers. They have blue stripes.
FERNANDO:	Silvia likes stripes.
CHORUS:	*Silvia likes stripes. She likes red. Which sneakers does Fernando like?*

◊   ◊   ◊

MYRA:	Which sneakers do you like?
FERNANDO:	I like those sneakers. I want the sneakers with red shoelaces. Silvia will like them.
SALESPERSON:	What shoe size do you need?
FERNANDO:	Oh, no! I don't know Silvia's shoe size!
CHORUS:	*Fernando doesn't know Silvia's shoe size. Oh, no!*
MYRA:	That's OK, Fernando. Silvia and I wear the same size!

Listen and Chant

WHAT will I WEAR?

It's sunny today.
What will I wear?
I'll wear these sandals
And the T-shirt over there.

Make your own chant.

gloves

windy

coat

snowy

boots

jacket

© NGSP & HB

227

Today is _____ .

230

Today is _____ .

228

Today is _____ .

231

Today is _____ .

229

Today is _____ .

232

Today is _____ .

230 Today is snowy.

231 Today is sunny.

232 Today is windy.

227 Today is cloudy.

228 Today is foggy.

229 Today is rainy.

Word File

WEATHER
Study and practice the words. Then check the words you use.

- ☐ **cloudy**
- ☐ **foggy**
- ☐ **rainy**
- ☐ **snowy**
- ☐ **sunny**
- ☐ **windy**

Find or draw more pictures of weather. Add them to your Word File.

- ☐ _____
- ☐ _____
- ☐ _____
- ☐ _____
- ☐ _____
- ☐ _____

Vocabulary

Describing Words

Use these words to describe the weather.

thermometer

hot   warm   cool   cold

wet

dry

👀 Look at each picture. 💬 Talk about the weather in the picture.

Say the words that finish each sentence. ✍️ Then write the words.

1

It's ___warm___ and ___sunny___ today.

2

It's _____ and _____ today.

3

It's _____ and _____ today.

Describe the Weather

💬 Work with a partner. Use your pictures. Point to a picture. Your partner describes the weather.

It's warm and sunny.

© NGSP & HB

Vocabulary

Weather and Describing Words

 Look at the weather forecast.

 Describe the weather on each day.

Then write the weather words in each sentence.

WORD BANK

cloudy	rainy
cold	snowy
cool	sunny
foggy	warm
hot	windy

Sunday

windy

cool

Monday

_____

_____

It's ___windy___ and ___cool___ today.

It's _____ and _____ today.

Tuesday	Wednesday	Thursday	Friday	Saturday

°F _____ °C (for each thermometer, scale reads 120, 100, 80, 60, 40, 20, 0, -20, -40 on left and 50, 40, 30, 20, 10, 0, -10, -20, -30, -40 on right)

It's _____ and _____ today.

It's _____ and _____ today.

It's _____ and _____ today.

It's _____ and _____ today.

It's _____ and _____ today.

Talk About the Weather

Work with a partner. Choose a day. Describe the weather to your partner. Take turns.

Express Ideas

Listen and Say

Use sentences like these to tell what you need, want, or have to do.

It's _____ today.	It's _____ today.	It's _____ today.
I need to _____ .	I want to _____ .	I have to _____ .

It's Cold and Snowy

Celia: It's cold and snowy today. I want to walk in the snow.

Yolanda: Great idea! But I need to find my boots. Where are they?

Celia: They're in the closet. I want to wear my warm coat.

Yolanda: I will wear my warm coat, too.

Celia: I have to wear a scarf.

Yolanda: Don't forget your hat and mittens!

Celia: OK. Let's go!

How It Works

Use **it's** with weather words and time and day words.

Weather	It's hot.	It's rainy.
Time and Day Words	It's 2:00.	It's Monday.

© NGSP & HB

Say and Write

 Look at each picture. Say the words that finish each sentence.

Then write the words.

1

It's ___snowy___ today.

I need to wear ___boots___ .

2

It's ___hot___ today.

I want to wear _____ .

3

_____ _____ today.

I _____ _____ wear a _____ .

4

_____ _____ today.

I _____ _____ wear a _____ .

5

_____ _____ _____ .

I _____ _____ wear a _____ .

6

_____ _____ _____ .

I _____ _____ wear a _____ .

On Your Own

 Work with a partner. Use your pictures.

Tell what the weather is like in each picture.

Talk about what you want, need, or have to wear.

It's sunny today.
I want to wear shorts.

Language Wrap-Up

Read and Retell

Build Background

Now you will read *What Should I Wear?* People wear different kinds of clothing for different reasons.

Read

As you read, learn why people wear special clothing.

Collect Words

You know many words for clothing. What new words did you learn in this book? Use the words to talk about the book.

Theme Book

CD 3 Track 21

What Should I Wear?

by Frank Hartley

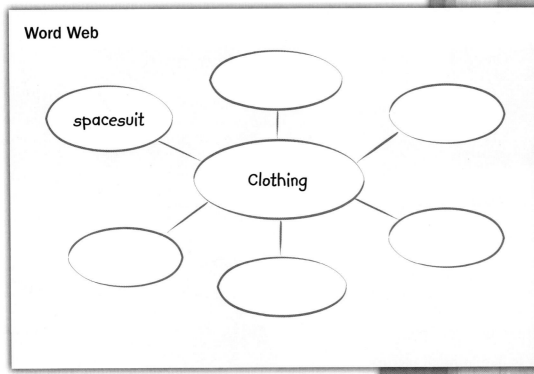

Word Web

spacesuit

Clothing

Tell About the Book

1 Think about the book. What is it mainly about?

> Reasons People Wear Special Clothing

2 Why do people wear special clothing? Write one reason.

> Reasons People Wear Special Clothing — to be safe

3 Who wears the clothing? Write words for people around each reason.

> Reasons People Wear Special Clothing — to be safe
> - astronaut
> - beekeeper
> - stunt person
> - firefighter

4 Now think of other reasons. Make your own concept map. Add your reasons to the map. Then write who wears the clothing.

Write a Letter and a List

February 10

Dear Hala,

I'm glad you are coming to Michigan soon. It's really cold here! Here is what you need to bring:

coat

gloves

hat

scarf

I can't wait to see you.

Your friend,
Noura

Focus on Sentences

A **statement** tells something. It ends with a **period**.

I am cold. < **period**

A sentence that shows strong feeling is called an **exclamation**. It ends with an **exclamation point**.

It's really cold here! < **exclamation point**

Write each sentence correctly. Add a period or an exclamation point.

1 It's really hot today

_____

2 I want to wear sandals

_____

3 It is rainy outside

_____

4 The wind is really cold

_____

Your friend is coming to visit you. Write a letter to your friend. Tell about the weather. Tell what clothes your friend needs to bring for the weather.

Dear _____ ,

    I'm glad you are coming to _____ soon. It's

_____ _____ .

Here is what you need to bring:

_____

_____

_____

_____

_____

_____

Your friend,

_____

Check Your Writing

Share your work with a partner. Check the writing. Did you put a period at the end of each statement? Did you put an exclamation point at the end of each exclamation?

Unit 9

Around Town

Unit Project

Draw a map of places in your community. Tell about places that are similar or different in your home country.

In This Unit

Try Out Language	Vocabulary	Language Function	Patterns	Language Wrap-Up	Writing
Chant	Community Places and Workers Location Words	Give Directions	*Where is the _____ ?* *Go _____ .* *Turn left at _____ .* *Turn right at _____ .* *The _____ is on _____ .* *It is _____ .* *The _____ is _____ the _____ .*	Language Game: Where Is the Post Office?	Write About Your Favorite Place
Chant	Community Places and Products Products for Sale	Express Intentions	*I am going to _____ .* *I will _____ .*	Theme Theater: A Day in Town	
Song	Vehicles Words for People	Describe Actions	*They ride _____ .* *They ride on a _____ .* *They ride in a _____ .* *They take _____ .*	Read and Retell **Getting from Here to There** Theme Book by Antonia Barber	

CD 3 Track 22

Listen and Chant

Walk
in the Community

Walk in the community.

Watch the people work.

Walk in the community.

Talk to a clerk.

Talk to a dentist

And a firefighter, too.

Talk to a doctor.

They are here to help you.

Make your own chant.

teller

police officer

cashier

mechanic

© NGSP & HB

Word File

COMMUNITY PLACES AND WORKERS

Check the words you know.

- ☐ bank
- ☐ teller
- ☐ community youth center
- ☐ instructor
- ☐ dentist's office
- ☐ dentist
- ☐ gas station
- ☐ mechanic
- ☐ hospital
- ☐ doctor
- ☐ nurse
- ☐ fire station
- ☐ firefighter
- ☐ police station
- ☐ police officer
- ☐ post office
- ☐ clerk
- ☐ restaurant
- ☐ waiter
- ☐ supermarket
- ☐ cashier

233

234

235

236

237

238

239

240

241

242

238 **fire station** — firefighter

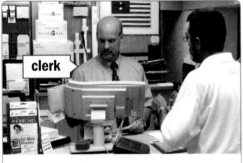

239 **police station** — police officer

240 **post office** — clerk

241 **restaurant** — waiter

242 **supermarket** — cashier

233 **bank** — teller

234 **community youth center** — instructor

235 **dentist's office** — dentist

236 **gas station** — mechanic

237 **hospital** — nurse, doctor

Word File

COMMUNITY PLACES AND WORKERS

Study and practice the words. Then check the words you use.

- [ ] **bank**
- [ ] **teller**
- [ ] **community youth center**
- [ ] **instructor**
- [ ] **dentist's office**
- [ ] **dentist**
- [ ] **gas station**
- [ ] **mechanic**
- [ ] **hospital**
- [ ] **doctor**
- [ ] **nurse**
- [ ] **fire station**
- [ ] **firefighter**
- [ ] **police station**
- [ ] **police officer**
- [ ] **post office**
- [ ] **clerk**
- [ ] **restaurant**
- [ ] **waiter**
- [ ] **supermarket**
- [ ] **cashier**

Find or draw more pictures of community places and workers. Add them to your Word File.

- [ ] _____
- [ ] _____
- [ ] _____

Vocabulary

Location Words

Use these words to tell where things are.

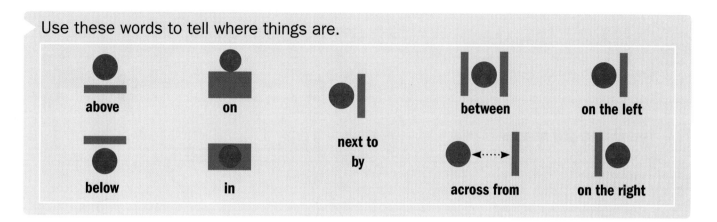

above

on

next to
by

between

on the left

below

in

across from

on the right

 Look at each picture. Say the words that finish each sentence.
 Then write the words.

1

The dentist's office is ___*between*___ the
restaurant and the bank.

3

The bank is _____ the supermarket.

The supermarket is _____ the bank.

2

The post office is _____ the
fire station.

Use Location Words

 Draw a simple map of places in
your community. Label the places.

Work with a partner.
Tell your partner where
the places are.

> The bank is next
> to the post office.

Vocabulary

Community Places and Workers

 Look at each picture.

 Say the name of each person and place.

 Then write the names.

WORD BANK

bank	instructor
cashier	mechanic
community youth center	nurse
dentist	police officer
dentist's office	police station
doctor	restaurant
firefighter	supermarket
fire station	teller
gas station	waiter
hospital	

2 The _____ works in the _____ .

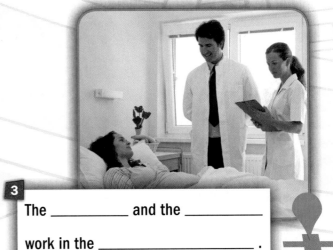

3 The _____ and the _____ work in the _____ .

1 The _____instructor_____ works in the __community youth center__ .

4 The _____ works in the _____ .

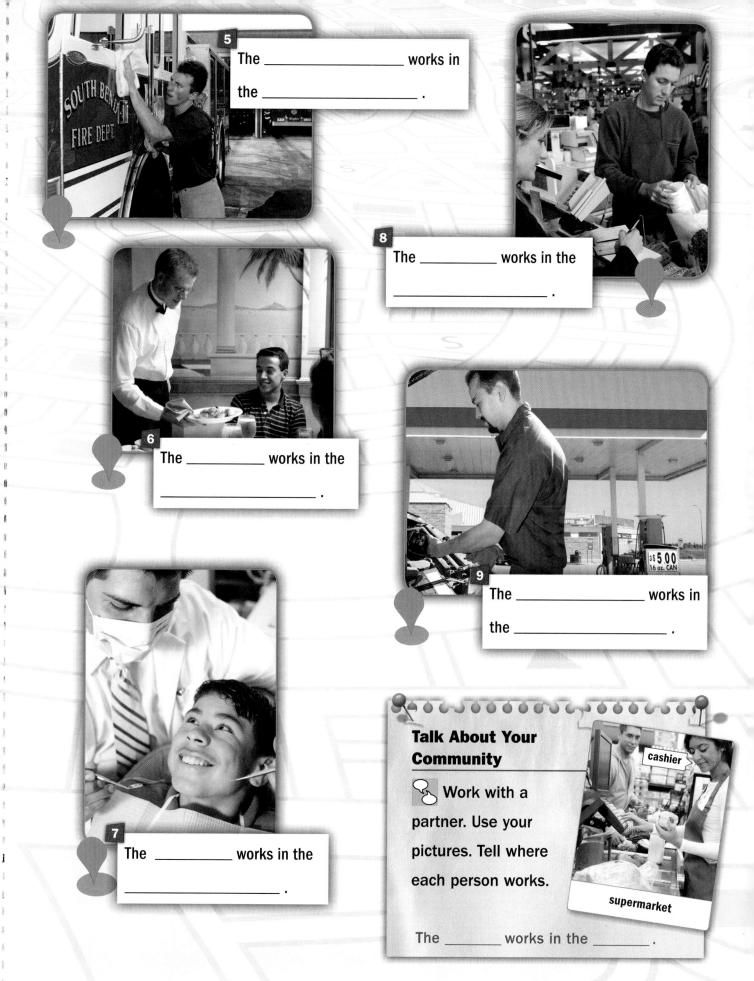

5 The _____ works in the _____ .

The _____ works in the _____ .

6 The _____ works in the _____ .

8 The _____ works in the _____ .

9 The _____ works in the _____ .

7 The _____ works in the _____ .

Talk About Your Community

Work with a partner. Use your pictures. Tell where each person works.

cashier

supermarket

The _____ works in the _____ .

Give Directions

CD 3 Track 23

Listen and Say

Use sentences like these to tell someone how to go to a place.

QUESTION	ANSWERS	
Where is the _____ ?	Go _____ . Turn left at _____ . Turn right at _____ .	The _____ is on _____ . It is _____ . The _____ is _____ the _____ .

Where Is the Post Office?

Scott: Excuse me. Where is the post office?

Jenny: Go down Main Street. Go one block. Turn left at the corner. Then turn right at First Street.

Scott: First Street?

Jenny: Yes. The post office is on First Street. It is next to the bank.

Scott: Thank you!

Jenny: You're welcome.

Use the Right Word

Use **at** or **on** to tell where a place is.

at	on
Use **at** if you know the exact address or place. The post office is **at** 17 First Street. Turn left **at** the corner.	Use **on** if you know just the street name in the address. The post office is **on** First Street.

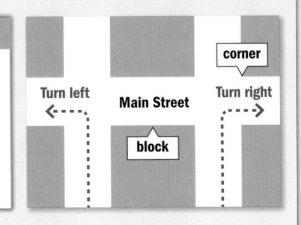

Say and Write

Look at the map. You are at the supermarket. Say the words that finish each sentence in the directions. Then write the words.

1 Where is the _____restaurant_____ ?

Go up _____First Street_____ .

Go _____ block. Turn

_____ at_____ .

The _____ is _____ the

dentist's office.

2 _____ _____ _____

bank?

Go one block on _____ .

The bank is at _____ .

It is _____ _____ the

police station.

On Your Own

Work with a partner. Ask your partner where a place is. Your partner tells you how to get there from the supermarket.

Where is the dentist's office?

Go up First Street. Turn right at Elm Street. The dentist's office is between the post office and the restaurant.

Language Wrap-Up

Play a Game

How to Play

1. Play with two other players.

 1   **2**   **3**

2. Player 1 chooses a place on the map. He or she asks for directions.

> Where is the post office?

3. Player 2 gives directions from the star to the place.

> Go down Seventh Street. Turn right on West Street. The post office is at 72 West Street.

4. If the directions are correct, Player 2 gets a point.

5. Then Player 2 asks for directions to a place. Player 3 gives directions.

6. The player with the most points wins.

Post Office
72 West Street

West Street

Dentist's Office
126 Eighth Street

Gas Station
108 Eighth Street

Eighth Street

Where Is the Post Office?

Police Station
105 Eighth Street

Hospital
76 Town Street

Seventh Street

Town Street

**Community
Youth Center**
62 Town Street

Bank
64 Lake Street

Supermarket
60 Lake Street

Lake Street

Fire Station
110 Sixth Street

Sixth Street

Restaurant
119 Sixth Street

Try Out Language

CD 3 Track 24

Listen and Chant

Going Shopping

I am going to buy some books.

I am going to buy some fruit.

I am going to buy some flowers.

I am going to buy some shoes.

I am going to buy some tickets.

I am going to buy some combs.

And when I finish shopping,

I am going to go home.

fruit

flowers

tickets

© NGSP & HB

282 Unit 9 | Around Town

Word File

COMMUNITY PLACES AND PRODUCTS

Check the words you know.

- [ ] **bookstore**
- [ ] **books**
- [ ] **clothing store**
- [ ] **caps**
- [ ] **flower shop**
- [ ] **flowers**
- [ ] **fruit stand**
- [ ] **apples**
- [ ] **hair salon**
- [ ] **combs**
- [ ] **hardware store**
- [ ] **hammers**
- [ ] **laundromat**
- [ ] **baskets**
- [ ] **movie theater**
- [ ] **tickets**
- [ ] **pharmacy**
- [ ] **thermometers**
- [ ] **shoe store**
- [ ] **shoes**

243

244

245

246

247

248

249

250

251

252

248 hardware store

hammers

243 bookstore

books

249 laundromat

baskets

244 clothing store

caps

250 movie theater

tickets

245 flower shop

flowers

251 pharmacy

thermometers

246 fruit stand

apples

252 shoe store

shoes

247 hair salon

combs

COMMUNITY PLACES AND PRODUCTS

Study and practice the words. Then check the words you use.

 □ bookstore

 □ books

□ clothing store

 □ caps

 □ flower shop

□ flowers

 □ fruit stand

 □ apples

 □ hair salon

□ combs

□ hardware store

□ hammers

□ laundromat

□ baskets

□ movie theater

□ tickets

□ pharmacy

□ thermometers

□ shoe store

□ shoes

Find or draw more pictures of community places and products. Add them to your Word File.

□ _____

□ _____

□ _____

□ _____

Vocabulary

Products for Sale

one

more than one

The name for more than one thing often ends in **-s**.

cap

caps

comb

combs

shoe

shoes

👓 **Look at the picture.** 💬 **Say the word for each item.** ✍️ **Then write the word. What items can you buy in a clothing store? Add -s for more than one.**

shirt

In a clothing store, you can buy some

1 ___shirts___ .

2 _____ .

3 _____ .

4 _____ .

5 _____ .

6 _____ .

Tell What You Can Buy

💬 Work with a partner. Use your pictures. Tell what you can buy in each place.

© NGSP & HB

Vocabulary

Community Places and Products

 Look at each picture.

Say the name of each place and each product.

Then write the name.

WORD BANK

apples	flower shop	movie theater
baskets	flowers	pharmacy
books	fruit stand	shoe store
bookstore	hair salon	shoes
caps	hammers	thermometers
clothing store	hardware store	tickets
combs	laundromat	

1. flowers

2. _____ flower shop _____

5. _____

6. _____

3. _____

4. _____

7. _____

8. _____

9

10 _____

15

16 _____

11

12 _____

17

18 _____

13

14 _____

19

20 _____

Talk About What You Can Buy

Work with a partner. Tell what you can buy in different stores.

I can buy some _____
at the _____ .

Listen and Say

Use sentences like these to tell what you plan to do.

I am going to _____ .	I will _____ .

This Weekend

Julie: What are you going to do on Saturday?

Cristina: I am going to buy some flowers at the flower shop. I will give them to my mom.

Julie: What else are you going to do?

Cristina: Then I am going to buy some shoes at the shoe store. I will wear them to the school dance.

Julie: You are so busy!

Cristina: What are you going to do this weekend?

Julie: I am going to act in a play. I will sing a song, too. Come and see me!

Cristina: Good idea! I will.

How It Works

CD 3 Track 26

Listen to these words. Listen for the **-s** at the end of each word. It means more than one. Now say the words with a partner. Be sure to say the **-s** at the end of each word.

basket**s**	apple**s**
book**s**	comb**s**
cap**s**	flower**s**
sock**s**	hammer**s**
ticket**s**	shoe**s**

Say and Write

 Look at each picture. Say the words that finish each sentence.
Then write the words.

1

I __am__ __going__ __to__ buy some apples.

I __will__ make an apple pie tomorrow.

3

I _____ _____ _____ buy some books.

_____ _____ read them this summer.

2

I __am__ _____ _____ buy some shoes.

I _____ wear them tonight.

4

_____ _____ _____ _____ buy some flowers.

_____ _____ give them to my mom for

her birthday.

On Your Own

Work with a partner. Use your pictures. Tell what you
are going to buy at each place. Use *I am going to* or *I will*.

> I am going to buy
> some tickets at
> the movie theater.

© NGSP & HB

Language Wrap-Up

CD 3 Track 27

Theme Theater

Yolanda and Oscar are going into town. They have many things to do. Listen to their conversation. Then act it out.

A DAY IN TOWN

OSCAR: What are you doing today, Yolanda?

YOLANDA: I am going to town.

OSCAR: What are you going to do?

YOLANDA: First, I am going to the post office. Then, I'm going shopping.

OSCAR: Can I come with you? I need to go to the library. I need to get a book for school.

YOLANDA: Yes, we can go to town together.

CHORUS: *Oscar and Yolanda are going to town. They have much to do.*

◊   ◊   ◊

YOLANDA: First, I will mail these letters.

OSCAR: OK. The fruit stand is on the corner. I am hungry. I am going to buy some apples. Meet me there.

YOLANDA: OK. See you at the corner.

CLERK: Can I help you?

YOLANDA: I want to mail these letters.

CLERK: That will be four dollars and twenty cents.

YOLANDA: Here you are.

CHORUS: *Oscar and Yolanda will meet at the corner.*

CHORUS

CLERK

YOLANDA

OSCAR

OSCAR: What are you going to do now?

YOLANDA: Now I am going to buy some combs at the hair salon.

OSCAR: I am going to the clothing store. I will buy a cap.

YOLANDA: Then we can see a movie.

OSCAR: Good idea. I will meet you at the movie theater. Then we will go to the library.

CHORUS: *Yolanda and Oscar will see a movie. Then they will go to the library.*

◈   ◈   ◈

OSCAR: That was a long movie. What time is it? I still need that book!

YOLANDA: There is the library.

OSCAR: Oh, no! The library is closed! I can't get the book!

YOLANDA: I feel bad! What will you do?

OSCAR: I will get it tomorrow.

YOLANDA: Good idea!

Listen and Sing

Go Downtown

You can take the bus or train

Or take the subway, too.

If you want to go downtown,

Any of those will do.

If you want to go downtown,

You'll need to pay a fare.

The bus, the train, or the subway,

They all will take you there.

292

NGSP & HB.

Word File

VEHICLES
Check the words you know.

- ☐ airplane
- ☐ ambulance
- ☐ bicycle
- ☐ bus
- ☐ car
- ☐ motorcycle
- ☐ skateboard
- ☐ subway
- ☐ taxi
- ☐ train

253

254

255

256

257

258

259

260

261

262

258 motorcycle

259 skateboard

260 subway

261 taxi

262 train

253 airplane

254 ambulance

255 bicycle

256 bus

257 car

Word File

VEHICLES

Study and practice the words. Then check the words you use.

- ☐ **airplane**
- ☐ **ambulance**
- ☐ **bicycle**
- ☐ **bus**
- ☐ **car**
- ☐ **motorcycle**
- ☐ **skateboard**
- ☐ **subway**
- ☐ **taxi**
- ☐ **train**

Find or draw more pictures of vehicles. Add them to your Word File.

- ☐ _____
- ☐ _____
- ☐ _____
- ☐ _____
- ☐ _____
- ☐ _____

Words for People

When you talk about more than one person, use **they**.
When you tell about what they own, use **their**.

My friends like to go places. **They** go everywhere.

They ride **their** bikes all day long.

 Look at each picture. Say the words that finish each sentence.
 Then write the words.

1

The students ride on ___their___ skateboards.

___They___ wear helmets.

2

The people drive _____ cars to work.

_____ do not want to be late.

3

My parents like to ride _____ motorcycles.

_____ go to visit family and friends.

Talk About Your Friends

Work with a partner. Tell how your friends go places. Talk about the vehicles they use.

My friends ride their bicycles. They ride to school. Their bicycles are new.

Describe Actions

Listen and Say

Use sentences like these to tell how people go places.

They ride _____ .	They ride on a _____ . They ride in a _____ .	They take _____ .

People go everywhere!
They ride bicycles.
They ride motorcycles.

They ride on a train.

They ride in a car.

They take the bus or the subway. They also take a taxi.

Use the Right Word

Use **in** or **on** when you talk about riding vehicles.

in	on	
Use **in** with these vehicles.	Use **on** with these vehicles.	
They ride **in** a car. I ride **in** an ambulance. We ride **in** a taxi. They ride **in** an airplane.	I ride **on** a skateboard. I ride **on** a bicycle. They ride **on** a motorcycle.	We ride **on** a bus. They ride **on** a train. I ride **on** the subway.

Say and Write

 Look at each picture. Say the words that finish the sentence.
Then write the words.

They ride ___bicycles___ .

They _____ _____ _____ car.

They ride ___on___ _____ _____ .

They _____ _____ .

They take _____ _____ .

They _____ a _____ .

On Your Own

Work with a partner. Talk about the vehicles on your picture cards from page 293. Use each picture. Make a sentence using *they ride* or *they take*.

They take the bus.

Language Wrap-Up

Read and Retell

Build Background

Now you will read *Getting from Here to There*. It is about how people around the world get to different places.

Read

As you read, find out about the different vehicles people use.

Collect Words

You know many words for vehicles. Write some of the words. What new words did you learn in this book? Use the words to talk about the book.

Theme Book

CD 3 Track 30

Getting from Here to There

by Antonia Barber

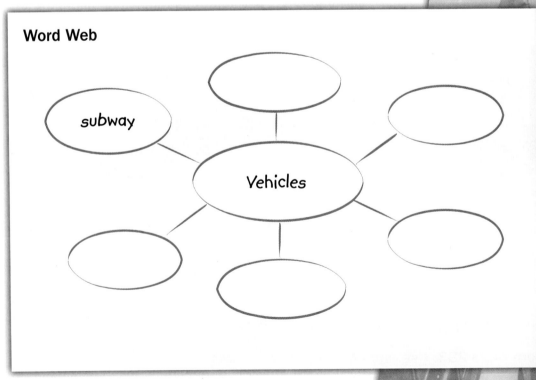

Word Web

- subway
- Vehicles

Tell About the Book

1 Think about the vehicles in *Getting from Here to There*. Write the name of each vehicle.

Vehicle	Places
subway	Tokyo, Japan
	Tokyo, Japan Mexico City, Mexico

2 Think about the places where people use these vehicles. Write the name of each place. Finish the chart.

3 Use your chart to tell a partner about vehicles around the world.

Write About Your Favorite Place

Study a Model

OAKVILLE YOUTH CENTER

I like the Oakville Youth Center. It is my favorite place.

I see Mr. Jones. He is a math tutor.

I talk with Eduardo. He is a good friend.

I take a picture with a camera.

Focus on Nouns

A **noun** names a person, place, or thing. Nouns add details to sentences. You can put **describing words** before nouns.

He is a **math tutor**.

| describing word | noun |

Describing Words	Nouns
big	day
green	map
rainy	notebook
science	teacher

Write the describing words and nouns that finish each sentence. Use the words in the chart on the left.

1 Today is a _____ _____ .

2 I have a _____ _____ .

3 He is a _____ _____ .

4 Look at the _____ _____

on the wall.

Write about your favorite place. Draw pictures to show people and activities at your favorite place.

Place: _____

I like _____ . It is my favorite place.

 Share your work with a partner. Check the writing.

Did you use nouns and describing words? Are your words in the right order?

Unit 10

All Year Long

Unit Project

Work with other students in your class. Make a class yearbook.

In This Unit

Try Out Language	Vocabulary	Language Function	Patterns	Language Wrap-Up	Writing
Song	Seasons, Months, and Activities Dates	Describe Actions	*In the _____, he _____.* *In _____, she _____.*	**Language Game:** Seasons of Fun	Write About a Celebration
Chant	Making Things Words for People	Describe Actions	*On _____, he _____.* *On _____, she _____.* *On _____, they _____.*	**Theme Theater:** The Party Problem	
Chant	Celebrations Words for People	Make a Request	*Will you please _____?* *Sure.* *May I _____?* *May we _____?* *Of course.*	**Read and Retell**	

Jari's Year
by Louise Franklin

Theme Book

Listen and Sing

Every Season of the Year

fall

Fall and winter, spring and summer,
Every season all year through,
There are lots of things we can do
That are fun for me and you.

winter

In September and October
And November, we have school.
In December, January,
February, snow is cool.

March and April and then May,
It's time to plant flowers again.
Then in June, July, and August,
Summer days should never end.

spring

summer

Fall and winter, spring and summer,
Every season all year through,
There are lots of things we can do
That are fun for me and you.

© NGSP & HB

Word File

SEASONS, MONTHS, AND ACTIVITIES
Check the words you know.

- ☐ winter
- ☐ spring
- ☐ summer
- ☐ fall
- ☐ sled down a hill
- ☐ plant seeds
- ☐ swim in a lake
- ☐ rake leaves
- ☐ month

263

267

264

268

265

269

266

270

Winter	**Spring**	**Summer**	**Fall**
December	March	June	September
January	April	July	October
February	May	August	November

267 sled down a hill

263 winter

268 plant seeds

264 spring

269 swim in a lake

265 summer

270 rake leaves

266 fall

Word File

SEASONS, MONTHS, AND ACTIVITIES

Study and practice the words. Then check the words you use.

- [ ] winter
- [ ] spring
- [ ] summer
- [ ] fall
- [ ] sled down a hill
- [ ] plant seeds
- [ ] swim in a lake
- [ ] rake leaves
- [ ] month

Find or draw more pictures of activities for each season. Add them to your Word File.

- [ ] _____
- [ ] _____
- [ ] _____
- [ ] _____
- [ ] _____
- [ ] _____

Winter	Spring	Summer	Fall
month ▷ December	March	June	September
January	April	July	October
February	May	August	November

Vocabulary

Dates

When you write or say a date, put the month first.

month	day	year

Write: **January 4, 2010**

↖ **Put a comma between the day and the year.**

Or write: **1/4/2010**

Say:

> January fourth, two thousand ten

👓 Look at each calendar. 💬 Say the date that is circled.

✍ Then write the date.

1

		NOVEMBER 2010				
Sunday	Monday	Tuesday	Wednesday	Thursday	Friday	Saturday
	1	2	3	4	5	6
7	8	9	10	11	12	13
14	(15)	16	17	18	19	20
21	22	23	24	25	26	27
28	29	30				

Today is _____November 15, 2010_____ .

3

		SEPTEMBER 2012				
Sunday	Monday	Tuesday	Wednesday	Thursday	Friday	Saturday
						1
2	3	4	5	6	7	8
9	10	11	12	13	14	15
16	17	18	19	20	21	22
23	24	25	26	27	(28)	29
30						

Today is _____ .

2

		JULY 2011				
Sunday	Monday	Tuesday	Wednesday	Thursday	Friday	Saturday
					(1)	2
3	4	5	6	7	8	9
10	11	12	13	14	15	16
17	18	19	20	21	22	23
24	25	26	27	28	29	30
31						

Today is _____ .

Say and Write Dates

💬 Work with a group. Say dates that are important to you. ✍ Write the dates. Tell the group about the dates and why they are important.

Describe Actions

Listen and Say

Use sentences like these to tell what people do in different seasons or months.

| In the fall, Tom _____ . | In the spring, Malia _____ . |
| In September, he _____ . | In April, she _____ . |

What Does Your Family Do?

Juan: Do people in your family do special things every season?

Oscar: Yes. My grandmother likes to bake. In September, she picks apples. Then she makes apple pies. What does your family do?

Juan: My father likes to work in the yard. In the spring, he plants flowers.

Oscar: My mother plants flowers in the spring, too!

How It Works

A **verb** can tell what a person does.

run   write   walk   jump

When you tell what one other person does, add **-s** to the verb.

Kam runs.

Alfredo writes.

She walks.

He jumps.

© NGSP & HB

Say and Write

 Look at each picture. Say the verb that finishes each sentence. Add -s to each verb. Then write the verb.

1

In the winter, he _shovels_ snow. (shovel)

2

In January, So Ying _____ . (skate)

3

In the spring, Tara _____ flowers. (plant)

4

In October, she _____ leaves. (rake)

5

In the summer, she _____ basketball. (play)

6

In July, he _____ in the pool. (swim)

On Your Own

 Work with a partner. Write what you do in each season. Change papers. Then tell the class what your partner does in each season.

> In the summer, Leticia runs. In September, she plays soccer.

Language Wrap-Up

Play a Game

How to Play

1. Play with a partner.

2. Use a coin.

3. Partner 1 tosses the coin onto the game board to make it land on an activity. Then Partner 1 tells when a family member or a friend does that activity.

> In the winter, my brother shovels snow.

4. If Partner 1 uses the correct verb with -s, he or she gets a point.

5. Then Partner 2 tosses a coin onto the game board to make it land on an activity.

6. Partners take turns. The winner is the first person to get five points.

Seasons of Fun

play basketball

skate

eat ice cream

shovel snow

pick apples

plant flowers

swim

rake leaves

ride a bicycle

Listen and Chant

PAPER ART

Measure the paper with a ruler.

Fold the paper up just right.

Cut the paper and make a design.

Put it up for the party tonight.

Word File

MAKING THINGS
Check the words you know.

- [ ] greeting card
- [ ] measure the paper
- [ ] ruler
- [ ] cut the paper
- [ ] fold the paper
- [ ] get the markers
- [ ] glue on a picture
- [ ] write a message
- [ ] put the card inside
- [ ] envelope
- [ ] write the address
- [ ] mail the card

271

271

272

_____ the paper

273

_____ the paper

274

_____ the paper

275

_____ the markers

276

_____ on a picture

277

_____ a message

278

_____ the card inside

279

_____ the address

280

_____ the card

276 glue on a picture

277 write a message

278 put the card inside

envelope

279 write the address

Carolina Gomez
137 Main S...
Spring, T...

280 mail the card

271 greeting card

HAPPY BIRTHDAY!

272 measure the paper

ruler

273 cut the paper

274 fold the paper

get the markers

275 get the markers

MAKING THINGS

Study and practice the words. Then check the words you use.

- ☐ **greeting card**
- ☐ **measure the paper**
- ☐ **ruler**
- ☐ **cut the paper**
- ☐ **fold the paper**
- ☐ **get the markers**
- ☐ **glue on a picture**
- ☐ **write a message**
- ☐ **put the card inside**
- ☐ **envelope**
- ☐ **write the address**
- ☐ **mail the card**

Find or draw more pictures of how to make things. Add them to your Word File.

- ☐ _____
- ☐ _____
- ☐ _____
- ☐ _____
- ☐ _____
- ☐ _____

Words for People

When you talk about people, use the right word.

he	she	they
Use **he** for one boy or one man.	Use **she** for one girl or one woman.	Use **they** for more than one person.

Look at each picture. **Write the word that finishes each sentence.**

1

It's Ricardo's birthday. ____He____ gets a gift.

2

It's Marc's birthday.

_____ has a special dinner.

3

Many people are at the party.

_____ dance to the music.

4

It's Lan's birthday. _____ eats cake.

5

It's Gabriela's birthday.

_____ wears a pretty dress.

Use Words for People

Work with a partner. Point to a picture on this page. Say the first sentence. Your partner says the second sentence.

Describe Actions

Listen and Say

Use sentences like these to tell what people do on different holidays.

On New Year's Day, Mom _____ .	On New Year's Day, Dad _____ .	On New Year's Day, my parents _____ .
On New Year's Day, she _____ .	On New Year's Day, he _____ .	On New Year's Day, they _____ .

Chinese New Year

Jean: When is Chinese New Year?

Ling: It's at the end of January or the beginning of February.

Jean: How do you celebrate the New Year?

Ling: My mother cooks a special meal. She makes it the night before. My brother likes to dance. On New Year's Day, he wears a lion costume and dances with a group.

Jean: Do *you* do anything special?

Ling: I visit my grandparents. They give me money in red envelopes!

How It Works

A **verb** can tell what a person does.	When you tell what one other person does, add **-s** to the verb.	When you tell what two or more people do, do not change anything.
cook	My aunt cooks.	My parents cook.
swim	She swims.	They swim.
play	My friend plays soccer.	My friends play soccer.
write	He writes stories.	They write stories.

© NGSP & HB

Say and Write

 Look at each picture. Say the words that finish each sentence.
Then write the words.

1

On New Year's Day, _she_ _dances_ .

(dance)

2

On Valentine's Day, _____ _____

cards. (give)

3

On New Year's Day, _____ _____

special clothes. (wear)

4

On Thanksgiving Day, _they_ _____

a big meal. (eat)

5

On Independence Day, _____

_____ the fireworks. (enjoy)

6

On Day of the Dead, _____ _____

special bread. (bake)

On Your Own

Work with a partner. Tell what you do on
different holidays. Then work with a group. Tell the
group what your partner does on different holidays.

> On New Year's Day,
> he eats special food.

317

Theme Theater

It is Kim's graduation day. Kim and her brother Loc are telling
Leila about her party. Listen to their conversation. Then act it out.

THE PARTY PROBLEM

LEILA: Congratulations, Kim! I made you a card.

KIM: Thank you.

LEILA: Will you have a graduation party?

KIM: Yes. We will have a party on Saturday.

LOC: It will be a family party only.

KIM: I want to have some friends at my party. But my mom says that will be too many people.

LOC: Our family is big!

CHORUS: *It is Kim's graduation day.*
She wants to have some friends at her party.

◈   ◈   ◈

LEILA: What do your parents usually do for a party?

KIM: My mom cooks special food. She is a great cook.

LEILA: What does your dad do?

KIM: My dad makes a cake. He decorates it with many colors.

CHORUS: *Kim's mom cooks for a party.*
Kim's dad bakes a cake.

LEILA: I think your party will be fun.

KIM: I want you to come to my party. I will ask my parents tonight.

LEILA: OK. See you tomorrow, Kim. Bye, Loc.

KIM: See you later, Leila.

LOC: Bye, Leila.

◊   ◊   ◊

[Kim opens the door.]

LOC: Surprise!

CHORUS: *Surprise!*

KIM: What is happening? All my friends are here.

LOC: It is a surprise party! Our family is here. All your friends are here, too.

LEILA: Loc talked to your mom and dad. He told them you wanted to have friends at your graduation party.

KIM: Thanks everyone. I'm so happy!

CHORUS: *Kim is happy.*
All her friends are
at the party.

319

Try Out Language

CD 3 Track 36

Listen and Chant

How You Celebrate

Tell me how you celebrate.

Do you march in a parade?

Do you dance or decorate

Or light candles on a cake?

Do you share a meal that's great?

Tell me how you celebrate.

Word File

CELEBRATIONS
Check the words you know.

- ☐ dance together
- ☐ decorate our home
- ☐ light candles
- ☐ make a cake
- ☐ march in a parade
- ☐ open a gift
- ☐ send a card
- ☐ share a meal
- ☐ wear special clothes
- ☐ wrap a present

281 _____ together

282 _____ our home

283 light _____

284 make a _____

285 march in a _____

286 open a _____

287 _____ a card

288 share a _____

289 _____ special clothes

290 _____ a present

286 open a gift

287 send a card

288 share a meal

289 wear special clothes

290 wrap a present

281 dance together

282 decorate our home

283 light candles

284 make a cake

285 march in a parade

CELEBRATIONS
Study and practice the words. Then check the words you use.

- ☐ dance together
- ☐ decorate our home
- ☐ light candles
- ☐ make a cake
- ☐ march in a parade
- ☐ open a gift
- ☐ send a card
- ☐ share a meal
- ☐ wear special clothes
- ☐ wrap a present

Find or draw more pictures of celebrations. Add them to your Word File.

- ☐ _____
- ☐ _____
- ☐ _____
- ☐ _____
- ☐ _____
- ☐ _____

Words for People

When you talk about people, use the right word.

I	you	we
Use **I** to talk about yourself.	Use **you** to talk to another person.	Use **we** to talk about yourself and another person.

 Look at each picture. Say the words that finish each sentence. Then write the words.

1 _I_ wear special clothes.

3 _____ dance together.

2 _____ play music.

Use Words for People

Work with a partner. Tell your partner what you and your family do to celebrate special days.

I send cards.

Make a Request

Listen and Say

Use a question like this to ask someone to do something.		Use questions like these to ask for something you want.		
QUESTION	**ANSWER**	**QUESTIONS**		**ANSWER**
Will you please _____ ?	Sure.	May I _____ ?	May we _____ ?	Of course.

The Cinco de Mayo Party

Arturo: Tomorrow is Cinco de Mayo. That's May 5. Are you coming to my party?

Miguel: Yes! I am excited about it.

Arturo: I need to decorate our home. Will you please help me?

Miguel: Sure. May I bring my cousin to the party? She is visiting from Mexico.

Arturo: Of course.

Miguel: May we bring some music?

Arturo: That will be great.

Miguel: See you tomorrow.

Arturo: Bye!

Use the Right Word

Use polite words for different reasons.

Excuse me.	Could I please . . .	Would you please . . .
Use **Excuse me** to get someone's attention.	Use **Could I please** to ask if you can do something.	Use **Would you please** to ask someone to do something for you.
Excuse me. Do you have the time?	**Could I please** use your calculator?	**Would you please** help me?

Say and Write

Look at each picture. Say the words that finish each question. Then write the words.

1

Will you please dance with me?

2

_____ _____ _____ make a cake?

3

_____ I _____ the gift now?

4

_____ _____ _____ _____ this meal?

5

_____ we _____ our home for the party?

6

_____ _____ _____ _____ this card?

On Your Own

Work with a partner. Take turns making requests about celebrations.

Will you please make a cake?

Sure.

325

Read and Retell

Build Background

Now you will read *Jari's Year*. Jari is from Nigeria. This is his first year in the United States.

Read

As you read, learn what Jari does each month of the year.

Collect Words

You know many words for activities and celebrations. What new words did you learn in this book? Write the words. Use the words to talk about the book.

Theme Book

CD 3 Track 38

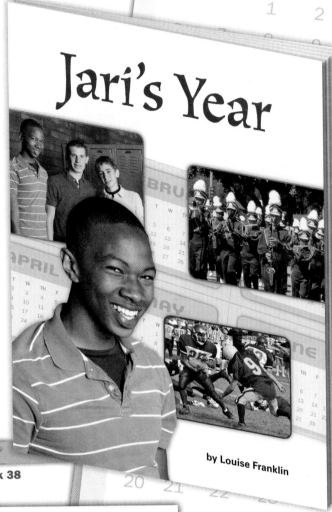

Jari's Year

by Louise Franklin

Word Web

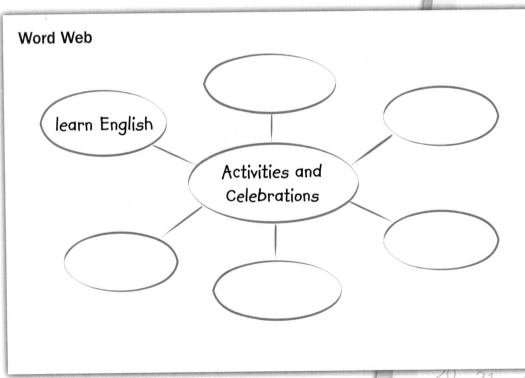

learn English

Activities and Celebrations

Tell About the Book

1 Think about *Jari's Year*. Write the name of each month.

2 Then write what Jari does in each month. Finish the chart.

Month	What Does Jari Do?
January	Jari learns English.

3 Use your chart to tell a partner about *Jari's Year*.

Write About a Celebration

Tet – The Vietnamese New Year
by Trong Pham

In January or February, we celebrate Tet.
For Tet, we do special things.

My father makes
special food.

We decorate our home
with flowers.

Focus on Verbs

A **verb** can tell what someone or
something does.

I We You They	**make** special food.

Add **-s** to the verb with **he**, **she**, and **it**.

He She	**makes** special food.
It	**makes** noise.

Finish each sentence. Write the verb
correctly.

1. We _____ cards for Valentine's Day. (make)

2. They _____ a meal on Thanksgiving. (share)

3. She _____ gifts in pretty paper. (wrap)

4. You _____ your home. (decorate)

5. He _____ special clothes for New Year's Day. (wear)

6. I _____ gifts on my birthday. (open)

Write about a celebration. Tell how you celebrate.

Draw pictures or tape some photos on this page.

_____

by _____

_____

_____

_____

_____

_____

_____

_____

 Share your work with a partner. Check the writing.

Did you use verbs correctly? Did you put -s at the end of

verbs for *he, she,* or *it*?

Acknowledgments

Illustrations

262-263, 265 (weather icons) Ken Batelman. 238 Cheryl Cook. 75-76 (cards 65-70) Jeff Fitz-Maurice. 202 Eric Hoffsten. 22-23, 56-57, 90-91, 128-129, 160-161, 192-193, 224-225, 256-257, 290-291, 318-319 Cedric Hohnstadt, Cedric Hohnstadt Illustration. 40-41, 178-179, 242-243 Terry Julian. 279 Jun Park.

Photographs

2 (bl) Masterfile (Royalty-Free Div.). (br) David Young-Wolff/PhotoEdit. (tl) PhotoAlto/Veer. (c) DigitalStock/Corbis (NGSP Image). 3 (t) Blend Images/Veer. (b) 2009 JupiterImages Corporation. (bg) Arlene Jean Gee/Shutterstock.com. (girl) David Young-Wolff/PhotoEdit. (frame) Solar/Shutterstock.com. 4 (cr) Jon Feingersh/AgeFotostock. (cl) Caroline Mowry/AgeFotostock. (bl) Charles Gupton/CORBIS. (bkgd) C. Devan/zefa/Corbis. 5 (l) Michael Newman/PhotoEdit. (tr) ImageState/Alamy. (br) Stewart Cohen/Blend Images/Jupiter Images. (br) Fancy/Veer/Corbis. (bkgd) iStockphoto.com/Paul Hart. 6 (tr) Liz Garza Williams. (tl) John Morrison/PhotoEdit. (bl) Corbis. (br) 2009 JupiterImages Corporation. (bkgd) 2008 © Melissa Evanko. Image from BigStockPhoto.com. 7 (bl) Chad McDermot/Fotolia. 8 (bl) Charlene Bayerle/Fotolia. (cr) Marmaduke St. John/Alamy. (br) JUPITERIMAGES/Creatas/Alamy. (tr) DesignPics Inc./Photolibrary. 9 (r) Randy Faris/Corbis. (cr) Lane Erickson/Fotolia. (b) Watt/Fotolia. 10 (cl) Davis Barber/PhotoEdit. 11 (tl) Ted Foxx/Alamy. (tr) Erik Isakson/Blend Images/Photolibrary. (r) iStockphoto.com/Herbert Bias. (cr) Myrleen Ferguson Cate/PhotoEdit. (b) Kevin Dodge/Corbis. 12 (l) Getty Images. (br) (C) 2006 © TongRo Image Stock. 13 (tl) Somos/Corbis. (tl) TongRo Image Stock/JupiterImages. (br) 2009 JupiterImages Corporation. (bl) David Young-Wolff/PhotoEdit. (c) Photodisc/Alamy. 14 (c) Simon Marcus/Corbis. (cl) ayimages/Alamy. 15 (tl) 2009 JupiterImages Corporation. (tl) Comstock/Corbis. (tl) UpperCut Images/Alamy. (tr) David Sacks/Getty Images. (br) JUPITERIMAGES/Brand X /Alamy. (cr) 2009 JupiterImages Corporation. (cr) MBI/Alamy. (c) 2009 JupiterImages Corporation. (bl) JUPITERIMAGES/Comstock Premium/Alamy. (br) Blend Images/Alamy. 16 (br) JUPITERIMAGES/Thinkstock/Alamy. (l) Comstock/Corbis. (cr) UpperCut Images/Alamy. (cl) David Sacks/Getty Images. (bl) JUPITERIMAGES/Brand X/Alamy. (cl) 2009 Jupiterimages Corporation. (cr) 2009 Jupiterimages Corporation. (bl) JUPITERIMAGES/Comstock Premium/Alamy. (bl) Blend Images/Alamy. (b) 2009 JupiterImages Corporation. 17 (tl) JUPITERIMAGES/Thinkstock/Alamy. (tl) Cindy Charles/PhotoEdit. (tr) Design Pics Inc./Alamy. (cl) Ariel Skelley/Blend Images/Getty Images. (bl) David Young-Wolff/PhotoEdit. (br) Spencer Grant/PhotoEdit. 18 (tl) Rob/Fotolia. (l) 2006 © lisafx. Image from BigStockPhoto.com. (tr) Michael Newman/PhotoEdit. (cr) David Young-Wolff/PhotoEdit. (cr) Daniel Montiel/Fotolia. (cl) 2009 Jupiterimages Corporation. (cl) Bonnie Kamin/PhotoEdit. (cr) Kayte Deioma/PhotoEdit. (br) 2006 © keeweeboy. Image from BigStockPhoto.com. (br) David Young/PhotoEdit. (bl) 2008 © Marmion. Image from BigStockPhoto.com . (bc) 2008 © Marmion. Image from BigStockPhoto.com. 19 (tl) David Young-Wolff/PhotoEdit. (tr) GoGo Images Corporation/Alamy. (b) Burstein Collection/CORBIS. (b) GoGo Images Corporation/Alamy. (br) David Young-Wolff/PhotoEdit. 20 (tl) Mike Kemp/Rubberball Productions/Getty Images. (br) David Young-Wolff/PhotoEdit. 21 (tr) Liz Garza Williams. (tl) NGSP. (cr) NGSP. (br) Creasource/Jupiter Images. 24 (c) DENKOU IMAGES GMBH. 25 (tl) Dmitry Kudryavtsev/Fotolia. (tr) Ariadne Van Zandbergen/Alamy. (tl) Peter Lievano/Fotolia. (tr) robert lerich/Fotolia. (cl) 2009 © belinda_bw. Image from BigStockPhoto.com . (cr) Richard Bickel/CORBIS. (bl) TEMISTOCLE LUCARELLI/Fotolia. (bl) Richard Wareham Fotografie/Alamy. (br) 2006 © Styve. Image from BigStockPhoto.com. 26 (tl) javarman. Image from BigStockPhoto.com. (tr) Alexey Stiop/Fotolia. (tl) Ken Welsh/age fotostock/Photolibrary. (tr) JosÈ Fuste Raga/zefa/Corbis. (bl) Can Balcioglu/Fotolia. (cr) Andrey Khrolenok/Fotolia. (bl) Martin Puddy/Asia Images/Jupiter Images. (br) 2007 © ragsac. Image from BigStockPhoto.com. (br) Holger Mette/Fotolia. 27 (t) 2007 © IndianSummer/Bigstock Photo.com. (r) W. Cody/CORBIS. (bl) W. Cody/CORBIS. (br) W. Cody/CORBIS. 28 (l) 2009 JupiterImages Corporation. (c) Rolf Bruderer/Blend Images/Photolibrary. (b) NGSP. (tr) Barbara Stitzer/PhotoEdit. 29 (br) 2008 © ajn. Image from BigStockPhoto.com. (br) Andrey Khrolenok/Fotolia. 30 (t) NGSP. (bkgd) 2009/Jupiterimages Corporation. 30-31 (c) Julie Flavin/Fotolia. (r) Peter Steiner/Alamy. (bg) Arlene Jean Gee/Shutterstock.com. (girl) David Young-Wolff/PhotoEdit. (frame) Solar/Shutterstock.com. 32 (l) Charles O. Cecil/Alamy. (l) Jeff Greenberg/PhotoEdit. (l) Charles O. Cecil/Alamy. (r) Sarah Hadley/Alamy. (r) Jeff Greenberg/PhotoEdit. (tl) Jeff Greenberg/PhotoEdit. (tl) Sarah Hadley/Alamy. 34. (bl) Banana Stock/Photolibrary. (tl) Philippe S. Giraud/Terres du Sud. 34-35 (c) 2009/Jupiterimages. 35 (t) Michael Newman/Photoedit. (br) RFR/Alamy. (tr) Photolibrary.

(m) Andersen Ross/Blend Images/Corbis. (bl) Staffan Tragardh/age footstock. (br) Mike McMillan - Spotfire Images. 36 (bkgd) amana images inc./Alamy. (br) 2006 © devon. Image from BigStockPhoto.com. (bl) MetaTools. (bc) SuperStock. (bl) 2007 © amorphis. Image from BigStockPhoto.com. (br) 2006 © devon. Image from BigStockPhoto.com. (c) Getty Images. (bl) Artville. 37 (tl) Suto Norbert/Fotolia. (tl) Brand X/Corbis. (cl) Getty Images. (b) 2006 © devon. Image from BigStockPhoto.com. (bl) JUPITERIMAGES/Brand X/Alamy. (tr) shinypix/Alamy. (tr) Artville. (br) Artville. (br) Retro Elite/Alamy. (tr) shinypix/Alamy. 38 (tr) Suto Norbert/Fotolia. (tl) Brand X/Corbis. (c) GettyImages. (br) 2006 © devon. Image from BigStockPhoto.com. (br) JUPITERIMAGES/Brand X/Alamy. (tr) shinypix/Alamy. (tl) Artville. (cl) Photodisc/Alamy. (bl) Getty Images. (bl) Retro Elite/Alamy. 39 (cl) 2006 © devon. Image from BigStockPhoto.com. (cl) 2007 © longlens. Image from BigStockPhoto.com. (tr) 2007 © homestudio. Image from BigStockPhoto.com. (tr) radarreklama/Fotolia. (bl) Getty Images. (br) Getty Images. (br) Feng Yu/Fotolia. (bl) SuperStock. (tr) RubberBall/Alamy. 40 (tr) Ian Shaw/Alamy. (cl) 2009 © Maggie1. Image from BigStockPhoto.com. (br) Getty Images. (bl) Getty Images. (bl) Metatools. 41 (bl) Artville. 42 (tl) PhotoAlto/Alamy. (tc) Scott B. Rosen/BSG/NGSP. (b) Suto Norbert/Fotolia. 43 (bl) MetaTools. (tc) 2008 © Dole. Image from BigStockPhoto.com. (tr) 2008 © ageshin. Image from BigStockPhoto. (cr) 2007 © homestudio. Image from BigStockPhoto.com. (bc) Getty Images. (c) 2009 © Maggie1. Image from BigStockPhoto.com. (bc) Feng Yu/Fotolia. 44 (tl) Getty Images. (cl) Getty Images. (cl) PhotoDisc/Getty Images. (tr) Artville. (tr) Getty Images. (tr) Getty Images. (cr) Getty Images. (c) 2006 © devon. (br) Artville. (bl) Artville. 45 (tl) Brand X/Corbis. (tc) Photodisc/Alamy. (c) Getty Images. (tr) Getty Images. (cr) 2006 © devon. Image from BigStockPhoto.com. (tl) NGSP. (br) MetaTools. 46 (c) Getty Images. (tr) Andres Rodriguez/Alamy. (b) David Young-Wolff/Alamy. (cr) 2007 © homestudio. Image from BigStockPhoto.com. (cr) MetaTools. (cr) SuperStock. (cr) Getty Images. (cr) 2006 © devon. Image from BigStockPhoto.com. (cr) Getty Images. (cr) 2008 © Robyn Mackenzie. Image from BigStockPhoto.com. 46-47 (bkgd) Jose Manuel Gelpi/Fotolia. 47 (tr) SuperStock. (bcl) 2008 © Robyn Mackenzie. Image from BigStockPhoto.com. (cl) Photodisc/Alamy. (bl) Artville. (cr) Getty Images. (br) 2006 © devon. Image from BigStockPhoto.com. (tl) MetaTools. (br) Getty Images. (br) 2007 © amorphis. Image from BigStockPhoto.com. (br) Getty Images. (br) GettyImages. 48 (bl) Spencer Grant/PhotoEdit. (br) Bill Aron/PhotoEdit. (bl) Dorling Kindersley/Getty Images. (br) Jupiterimages. (c) 2009/JupiterImages. 49 (tl) Kimberly Reinic/Fotolia. (tl) yang yu/Fotolia. (cl) design56/Fotolia. (bl) Jupiterimages. (b) Getty Images. (tr) 2006 © Canadian Loon> Image from BigStockPhoto.com. (cr) Steve Hamblin/Alamy. (cr) Getty Images. (br) 2008 © benkeuken2005. Image from BigStockPhoto.com. (br) moodboard/Corbis. 50 (tr) Kimberly Reinick/Fotolia. (tr) yang yu/Fotolia. (br) design56/Fotolia. (br) Jupiterimages. (br) Getty Images. (tl) 2006 Canadian Loon. Image from BigStockPhoto.com. 50. (tl) Steve Hamblin/Alamy. (cl) Getty Images. (bl) 2008 © benkeuken2005. Image from BigStockPhoto.com. 50. (bl) moodboard/Corbis. 51 (tl) Jupiterimages. (tl) Photodisc/Alamy. (bl) Bill Aron/PhotoEdit. (br) Dorling Kindersley/Getty Images. (tr) Spencer Grant/PhotoEdit. (cr) David Young-Wolff/PhotoEdit. (tr) Steve Skjold/Alamy. 52-53 (b) Michael Newman/PhotoEdit. (b) (tc) Ryan Mcvay/Getty Images. (br) Spencer Grant/PhotoEdit. (br) Dorling Kindersley/Getty Images. 54 (cl) George Doyle. (tr) NGSP. (cr) NGSP. (cr) Pedro Díaz/Fotolia. (b) Elnur/Fotolia. (tr) Kimberly Reinick/Fotolia. (b) 2009 JupiterImages Corporation. (tl) 2007 © xxabi. Image from BigStockPhoto.com. (tl) NGSP. 55 (c) Spencer Grant/PhotoEdit. (br) 2008 © Nik_Sorokin. Image from BigStockPhoto.com 58. (cl) Picture Partners/Alamy. (c) Kinn Deacon/Alamy. (bl) Visions of America, LLC/Alamy. (br) 2006 © Canadian Loon.Image from BigStockPhoto.com. (tr) Kathy deWitt/Alamy. (r) Purestock/Alamy. (bl) Visions of America, LLC/Alamy. 59 (t) RFR/Alamy. (tl) PhotoDisc/Getty Images. (cl) Andersen Bross/Blend Images/Jupiterimages. (bl) Dan Forer/Beateworks/Corbis. (tr) Liz Garza Williams. (tr) PhotoDisc/Getty Images. (br) Photos.com/Jupiterimages. (br) Andre Jenny/Alamy. (bl) Benjamin Rondel/Alamy. (br) Mike Powell/Getty Images. 60 (tr) RFR/Alamy. (tr) PhotoDisc/Getty Images. (cl) Andersen Bross/Blend Images/Jupiterimages. (br) Dan Forer/Beateworks/Corbis. (tl) Liz Garza Williams. (tl) PhotoDisc/Getty Images. (cl) Photos.com/Jupiterimages. (bl) Andre Jenny/Alamy. (br) Benjamin Rondel/Alamy. (bl) Mike Powell/Getty Images. 61 (tl) Dennis MacDonald/Alamy. (tr) Tom Grill/Corbis. (tl) Photodisc/Alamy. (br) Edward Green/Alamy. (cl) Syracuse Newspapers/Stephen Cannerelli/The Image Works. (cr) Masterfile (Royalty-Free Div.). (bl) John Cooper/Alamy. (br) 2007 © gizmo. Image from BigStockPhoto.com. (bl) Tammy Mobley/Fotolia. (br) 2007 © stvan4245. Image from BigStockPhoto.com. 62 (cl) Dennis MacDonald/Alamy. (tr) Tom Grill/Corbis. (tr) Photodisc/Alamy. (tl) Richard Green/Alamy. (cr) Syracuse Newspapers/Stephen

Cannerelli/The Image Works Image. (cl) Masterfile (Royalty-Free Div.). (br) John Cooper/Alamy. (bl) 2007 © gizmo. Image from BigStockPhoto.com. (br) Tammy Mobley/Fotolia. (b) 2007 © stvan4245, Image from BigStockPhoto.com. 63 (b) RFR/Alamy. (inset) Andre Jenny/Alamy. 64 (b) Syracuse Newspapers/Stephen Cannerelli/The Image Works. (br) William Whitehurst/CORBIS. 65 (t) John Cooper/Alamy. (br) 2007 © stvan4245. Image from BigStockPhoto.com. 66 (tl) Getty Images. (tc) 2008 © rob@enteravalon. Image from BigStockPhoto.com. (tr) Getty Images. (bc) 2009 Jupiterimages Corporation. (cr) Getty Images. (bl) Kathy deWitt/Alamy. (br) Masterfile (Royalty-Free Div.). 67 (cl) 2009 Jupiter Images Corporation. (cl) Masterfile (Royalty-Free Div.). (tc) UpperCut Images/Alamy. (c) Blend Images/Alamy. (tr) 2006 © Tupungato. Image from BigStockPhoto.com. (cr) David Young-Wolff/PhotoEdit. 68 (spread) 2008 © Mark Winfrey. Image from BigStockPhoto.com. (tr) NGSP. 70 (cl) Peter Steiner/Alamy 72 (bl) Ableimages/Photolibrary. (t) Sandra Cunningham/Shutterstock.com. (r) Chris Cinton/Taxi/Getty Images. (bl) Photos.com/Jupiterimages. 73 (t) Photo Network/Alamy. (b) Gary Conner/PhotoEdit. (fg) Photolibrary. (bg) Betacam-SP/Shutterstock.com. (mr) Michael Newman/PhotoEdit. (mr) Cindy Charles/PhotoEdit. (br) Ariel Skelley/Corbis. 74 (r) Darius Ramazani/zefa/Corbis. (bl) 2006 © pkruger. Image from BigStockPhoto.com. (bc) 2006 © pkruger. Image from BigStockPhoto.com. (bkgd) 81A Productions/Photolibrary. (l) PhotoAlto/Laurence Mouton/Jupiter Images 77. (l) 2006 © pkruger. Image from BigStockPhoto.com. (l) 2006 © pkruger. Image from BigStockPhoto.com. (c) 2006 © c pkruger. Image from BigStockPhoto.com. (c) 2006 © pkruger. Image from BigStockPhoto.com. (r) 2006 © pkruger. Image from BigStockPhoto.com. (r) 2006 © pkruger. Image from BigStockPhoto.com. (cl) 2008 © hartlandmartin.Image from BigStockPhoto.com. (cl) 2008 © volk65. Image from BigStockPhoto.com. (cr) intelwebs/Fotolia. (bl) HP_Photo/Fotolia. (bc) JUPITERIMAGES/Comstock Images/Alamy. 78 (tl) Ed Kashi/Corbis. (cl) Index Stock Imagery/Photolibrary. (cl) 2009 Jupiterimages Corporation. (bl) 2009 Jupiterimages Corporation. (tr) Tom Stewart/CORBIS. (bcr) David R. Frazier Photolibrary, Inc./Alamy. (br) Masterfile. (cr) Image Source/Corbis. (tr) 2006 © pkruger. Image from BigStockPhoto.com. (tcr) 2006 © pkruger. Image from BigStockPhoto.com. (bcr) 2006 © pkruger. Image from BigStockPhoto.com. (br) 2006 © pkruger. Image from BigStockPhoto.com. 79 (tl) 2009 Jupiterimages Corporation. (cl) Ian Shaw/Alamy. (bl) Galina Barskaya/Fotolia. (tc) 2008 © jaboardm. Image from BigStockPhoto.com. (c) 2009 Jupiterimages Corporation. (c) Getty Images. (cr) Blend Images/Alamy. 80 (l) Onidji/Fotolia. (cl) 81A Productions/Photolibrary. (r) JUPITERIMAGES/Creatas/Alamy. (br) Corbis Super RF/Alamy. 81 (tl) amridesign/Fotolia. (cl) 2005 © Hank Shiffman. Image from BigStockPhoto.com. (tr) JUPITERIMAGES/Creatas/Alamy. (bc) Brand X Pictures/Photolibrary. 82 (tl) Artville NGSP. (br) Roy Botterell/Corbis. (bl) 2006 © pkruger. Image from BigStockPhoto.com. 83 (bkgd) William Whitehurst/Corbis. (b) 2006 © pkruger. Image from BigStockPhoto.com 84 (br) 2009 Jupiterimages Corporation. (bl) Liz Garza Williams. (t) Somos Images LLC/Alamy. 85 (tl) Terry Vine/Getty Images. (cl) Simon Jarratt/Corbis. (cl) Dynamic Graphics. All rights reserved.. (bl) Corbis. (cl) Jose Luis Pelaez Inc/Getty Images. (cr) Chris Cinton/Taxi/Getty Images. (br) Image Source/Corbis. (br) 2009 Jupiterimages Corporation. 86 (tl) Terry Vine/Blend Images/Getty Images. (tl) Simon Jarratt/Corbis. (cl) Dynamic Graphics. All rights reserved. (bl) Corbis. (tr) Jose Luis Pelaez Inc/Blend Images/Getty Images. (tr) Chris Clinton/Taxi/Getty Images. (cr) Image Source/Corbis. (br) 2009 Jupiterimages Corporation. 87 (br) 2006 © pkruger, Image from BigStockPhoto.com. 88 (tl) Masterfile (Royalty-Free Div.). (tr) David Young-Wolff/PhotoEdit. (br) Onidji/Fotolia. 89 (br) Ian Shaw/Alamy 92. (t) Photolibrary RF. (bl) Aaron Haupt/Photo Researchers, Inc.. (bl) Billy E. Barnes/PhotoEdit. (c) Kinn Deacon/Alamy. (bcr) David Mendelsohn/Masterfile. (bkgd) Photodisc/Alamy. 93 (tl) ASSOCIATED PRESS. (bkgd) Lon C. Diehl/PhotoEdit. (cl) Fancy/Veer/Corbis. (bl) David Young-Wolff/PhotoEdit. (bl) David Young-Wolff/PhotoEdit. (tr) Jupiterimages. (tr) Alamy Images. (r) Michael Newman/PhotoEdit. (br) Mary Kate Denny/PhotoEdit. (br) Picture Contact/Alamy. (inset) JUPITERIMAGES/Creatas/Alamy. 94 (tl) ASSOCIATED PRESS. (inset) JUPITERIMAGES/Creatas/Alamy. (cl) Fancy/Veer/Corbis. (bl) David Young-Wolff/PhotoEdit. (b) Copyright David Young-Wolff/PhotoEdit. (br) 2009 Jupiterimages Corporation. (tr) Alamy Images. (cr) Michael Newman/PhotoEdit. (br) Mary Kate Denny/PhotoEdit. (br) Picture Contact/Alamy. (bkgd) Lon C. Diehl/PhotoEdit. 95 (t) Masterfile (Royalty-Free Div.). (b) Martin Mayer/Alamy. 96 (tl) Aaron Haupt/Photo Researchers, Inc.. (b) Picture Contact/Alamy. 97 (t) Ian Shaw/Alamy. (b) Spencer Grant/PhotoEdit. 98 (t) Michael Chamberlin/Fotolia. (b) SuperStock. 99 (bkgd) Wolfram Schroll/zefa/Corbis. (inset) Michael Newman/PhotoEdit. (b) 2009

330

Jupiterimages Corporation. **100** (l) RubberBall/SuperStock. (r) Image Source/Getty Images. **102** (tcl) Michael Newman/PhotoEdit. (cl) PhotoDisc/Getty Images. (bcl) Jupiterimages. (tr) Corbis. (cr) Digital Vision/Getty Images. (bcr) Getty Images. **103** (l) David Young-Wolff/PhotoEdit. (cr) Custom Medical Stock Photo/Alamy. (cl) Itani/Alamy. (r) 2007 © lisafx. Image from BigStockPhoto.com. (br) Blend Images/Photolibrary. **104** 2008© Cathy Yeulet. Image from BigStockPhoto.com (fg) Photolibrary. (bg) Betacam-SP/Shutterstock.com; (tl) Michael Newman/PhotoEdit; (mr) Cindy Charles/PhotoEdit; (br) Ariel Skelley/Corbis. **106** (tl) Corbis. (cl) 2008© Mark Winfrey. Image from BigStockPhoto.com. **108.** (tl) 2008 © Hathaway, Image from BigStockPhoto.com. (r) Styley/PYMCA/Jupiterimages. (bl) Somos Images/Corbis. **109** (t) Corbis. (tr) Corbis. (b) studiomode/Alamy. (br) Mitch Kloorfain. **110** (bl) Jonathan Nourok/PhotoEdit. (bcl) Blend Images/Alamy. (bcr) imagebroker/Alamy. 2009/Jupiterimages Corporation. (tc) Michael Newman/PhotoEdit. **111** 2009/Jupiterimages Corporation. (tl) 2009/Jupiterimages Corporation. (cl) Andrew Fox /Alamy. (cl) Blend Images/Alamy. (bl) imagebroker/Alamy. (bl) Monkey Business/Fotolia. (tr) 2009/Jupiterimages Corporation. (tr) 2009/Jupiterimages Corporation. (cr) Masterfile (Royalty-Free Div.). (br) 2009 /Jupiterimages Corporation. (br) 2009/JupiterImages Corporation. (tl) 2009/Jupiterimages Corporation. (tl) Andrew Fox/Alamy. (cl) Blend Images/Alamy. (bl) Monkey Business/Fotolia. 2009/Jupiterimages Corporation. (tr) 2009/Jupiterimages Corporation. (cr) Masterfile (Royalty-Free Div.). (br) 2009/Jupiterimages Corporation. (br) 2009/Jupiterimages Corporation **113.** (tl) UpperCut Images/Alamy. (tr) ImageState/Alamy. (cl) Purestock/Alamy. (bl) 2009/Jupiterimages Corporation. (br) Comstock Images/Jupiterimages. **114** (l) 2009/Jupiterimages Corporation. (c) 2009/JupiterImages Corporation. (br) Masterfile (Royalty-Free Div.). (br) Colin Young-Wolff/PhotoEdit. **115** (c) GlowImages/Alamy. (bc) Michael Newman/PhotoEdit. (br) ilian people/Alamy. **114-115.** (tr) 2009/Jupiterimages Corporation. **116** (tl) Comstock Images/Jupiterimages. (cl) Richard G. Bingham II/Alamy. (tr) David Young-Wolff/PhotoEdit. (cr) 2009/Jupiterimages Corporation. (br) Stockbyte/Alamy. **117** (tl) Bill Bachman/PhotoEdit. **118.** (cl) Artville. (tl) Artville. (bc) Photodisc/Alamy. (cl) pixland/Corbis. (br) Photodisc/Alamy. (cl) pixland/Corbis. **119** (r) pixland/Corbis. **120** (tl) 2008 © moori . Image from BigStockPhoto.com. (bkgd) PhotoLibrary. (bcl) iStockphoto.com/RBFried. (bcr) Tom Grill/Corbis. (bcr) 2006 © nruboc. Image from BigStockPhoto.com. (bl) Michele Westmorland/CORBIS. **121** (tl) 2007© ScovoPhoto.Image from BigStockPhoto.com. (tl) iStockphoto.com/Generistock. (cl) iStockphoto.com/RBFried. (bl) 2008 © Andreas Gradin. Image from BigStockPhoto.com. (bl) PhotoLibrary. (br) 2006 © nruboc.Image from BigStockPhoto.com. (tr) Stockbyte/Alamy. (cr) iStockphoto.com/TommL. (br) 2007 © Alex Bramwell.Image from BigStockPhoto.com. **122** (tr) 2007 © ScovoPhoto.Image from BigStockPhoto.com. (r) iStockphoto.com/Generistock. (tr) iStockphoto.com/RBFried. (br) 2008 © Andreas Gradin. Image from BigStockPhoto.com. (br) PhotoLibrary. (tl) 2006 © nruboc.Image from BigStockPhoto.com. (tl) Stockbyte/Alamy. (cl) iStockphoto.com/TommL. 2007 © Alex Bramwell.Image from BigStockPhoto.com. (bl) Tom Grill/Corbis. **123.** (tr) Tom Grill/Corbis. (tc) David Young-Wolff/PhotoEdit. (bl) Richard Hutchings/CORBIS. (c) 2008 © arturoli, Image from BigStockPhoto.com. (bc) 2008 Hathaway, Image from BigStockPhoto.com. (c) Alamy Images. (tr) Liz Garza Williams. (tl) David Young-Wolff/PhotoEdit. **124** (tl) Picture Contact/Alamy. (tc) 2009/Jupiterimages Corporation. (tr) D. Hurst/Alamy. (bl) Image Source Black/Alamy. (bc) Masterfile (Royalty-Free Div.). (br) 2007 © AleksandrL Image from BigStockPhoto.com. **125** (cl) moodboard/Corbis. (bl) 2007 © robophobic. Image from BigStockPhoto.com. (bc) Masterfile (Royalty-Free Div.). (br) Blend Images/Alamy. (br) Stockbyte/SuperStock. Copyright Lon C. Diehl/PhotoEdit. **126** (tl) David Woods/CORBIS. (br) Photodisc/Alamy. **127** (tl) Rick Gomez/Masterfile. (cl) Corbis RF/Alamy. (tr) Al Fuchs/NewSport/Corbis. (br) Juniors Bildarchiv/Alamy. (br) 2009/Jupiterimages Corporation **130.** (inset) Masterfile (Royalty-Free Div.). **131** (tl) Bob Daemmrich/The Image Works. (tl) Gideon Mendel/Corbis. (cl) ALAN ODDIE/PhotoEdit. (bl) Ellen Senisi/The Image Works. (bl) Tom Carter/PhotoEdit. (tr) Fancy/Veer/Corbis. (tr) Digital Vision/Alamy. (cr) Cindy Charles/PhotoEdit. (br) arabianEye/Getty Images. (br) Image Source Black/Alamy. **132** (tl) Bob Daemmrich/The Image Works. (tl) Gideon Mendel/Corbis. (cl) ALAN ODDIE/PhotoEdit. (bl) Ellen Senisi/The Image Works. (bl) Tom Carter/PhotoEdit. (tr) Fancy/Veer/Corbis. (tr) Digital Vision/Alamy. (cr) Cindy Charles/PhotoEdit. (br) arabianEye/Getty Images. (br) Image Source Black/Alamy. **133** (tl) Cleve Bryant/PhotoEdit. (tcl) Michael Newman/PhotoEdit. (bcl) Bonnie Kamin/PhotoEdit. (bl) Jake Hellbach/jutta klee/Ableimages/Photolibrary. (bcr) Masterfile (Royalty-Free Div.). (tr) Thinkstock Images/Jupiterimages. (cl) Stephen Coburn/Fotolia. (tr) Asia Selects/Photolibrary. **134** (tl) Russell Glenister/image100/Corbis. (cl) Golden Pixels LLC/Alamy. (tc) Annette Coolidge/

PhotoEdit. (c) Thinkstock/Corbis. (tr) Stockbyte/Getty Images. (tr)Stockbyte/Getty Images. (bcl) Ariel Skelley/Blend Images/Corbis. (cr) iStockphoto.com/WebSubstance. **135.** (bkgd) Jim Lane/Alamy. (bl) Sara Danielsson/Etsa/Corbis. (tl) Images-USA/Alamy. (tr) Brand X Pictures/Photolibrary. (c) Creatas/Photolibrary. (r) Getty Images. **136** (tl) Image Source/Corbis. (br) GettyImages. **137** (tl) Masterfile (Royalty-Free Div.). (br) Blend Images/Alamy. (br) LatinStock Collection/Alamy. (tr) Janine Wiedel Photolibrary/Alamy. (cl) Danita Delimont/Alamy. (b) Simon Marcus/Corbis. (bl) Stuart Cohen/The Image Works. (bc) Getty Images. **138** (tr) NGSP. **138-139.** (bkgd) Picture Contact/Alamy. **140** (tl) Sean Ellis/Getty Images. (tr) Mitch Kloorfain. **142.** (tl) Jupiterimages. (bl) Anne Ackermann/Getty Images. (bl) dmac/Alamy. (bc) Visions LLC/Photolibrary.com. (bl) Artville. (br) Image Club. **142-143.** (c) Tracey Kusiewicz/Foodie Photography/Jupiterimages. **143** (br) Martin Jacobs/Jupiterimages. (tr) Virgo Productions/zefa/Corbis. **144** (tr) iStockphoto.com/Dan Chippendale. (c) Digital Vision/Alamy. (bl) Artville. (c) iStockphoto.com/Stefanie Timmermann. (c) Planet Art. (bc) Artville. (cl) iStockphoto.com/bluestocking. (b) Brand X Pictures/Jupiterimages. **145** (cl) Stockbyte/Getty Images. (bl) JUPITERIMAGES/Brand X/Alamy. (br) SuperStock. (b) iStockphoto.com/Steven von Niederhausern. (cr) Foodcollection RF/Getty Images. (tr) Value Stock Images/Unlisted Images. (tr) Jupiterimages. (bcr) Getty Images. (tr) Jupiterimages. (b) Artville. (tl) Iconotec. **146** (tr) Value Stock Images/Unlisted Images. (tr) iStockphoto.com/Steven von Niederhausern. (tr) Iconotec. (tr) Brand X Pictures/Jupiterimages. (cl) John A. Rizzo/Getty Images. (cl) Foodcollection RF/Getty Images. (cl) Stockbyte/Getty Images. (bl) SuperStock. (br) Artville. (b) Getty Images. (br) JUPITERIMAGES/Brand X/Alamy. **147** (tr) iStockphoto.com/DNY59. (tl) iStockphoto.com/MorePixels. (t) iStockphoto.com/Klaudia Steiner. (c) iStockphoto.com/jerryhat. (t) PhotoAlto/Alamy. (tr) iStockphoto.com/Steven von Niederhausern. (br) CreativeAct - Abstract series/Alamy. **148** (tl) MetaTools. (l) iStockphoto.com/bedo. **148-149.** (c) Ilene MacDonald/Alamy Images. **149** (b) PhotoDisc/Getty Images. (b) Jupiterimages. **150** (tl) NGSP. (tr) NGSP. (tc) MetaTools. (br) PhotoDisc/Getty Images. (tr) Photodisc/Alamy. **151** (cr) FoodCollection/StockFood America. (tl) C Squared Studios/Photodisc/Getty Images. (cl) Artville. (c) NGSP. (bc) Grove Pashley/Getty Images. (cl) NGSP. (c) iStockphoto.com/jerryhat **154** (tr) PhotoDisc/Getty Images. (cr) Westend61/Alamy. (bl) Artville. (br) Photodisc/Getty Images. (tc) Artville. (bl) Corbis. (bc) PhotoDisc/Getty Images. (br) Comstock Images/Jupiterimages. (tr) PhotoDisc/Getty Images. **155** (bl) Corbis. (br) Artville. (tr) David Young-Wolff/PhotoEdit. (tl) Image Source/Corbis. (bl) Sean Justice/Corbis. (b) Artville. **156** (tr) Image Source/Corbis. (tl) PhotoDisc/Getty Images. (tr) PhotoDisc/Getty Images. (tl) David Young-Wolff/PhotoEdit. (cl) New Century Graphics. (bl) Artville. (br) Sean Justice/Corbis. (br) Corbis. (bl) Comstock Images/Jupiterimages. **157** iStockphoto.com/bluestocking. (tl) iStockphoto.com/Marie-france Bélanger. (br) iStockphoto.com/Bart Broek. (bl) iStockphoto.com/artesign. (c) Mauritius Images/Photolibrary.com. (b) iStockphoto.com/Jason Lugo. (b) iStockphoto.com/Floortje. (b) iStockphoto.com/Julie Deshaies. (cr) JanFo/Alamy. (cr) iStockphoto.com/artesign. (cl) iStockphoto.com/Karin Lau. **158** (cl) Paul Barton/CORBIS. (cl) Paul Barton/CORBIS. **159** (cl) Stockbyte/Photolibrary.com. (b) Purestock/Alamy **162** (tl) Foodcollection RF/Getty Images. (c) Yellow Dog Productions/Getty Images. **163** (cr) Brand X/Corbis. (br) Artville. (bl) Visions of America, LLC/Alamy. (c) Alan Schein Photography/CORBIS. (tl) Artville. (cl) Ilene MacDonald/Alamy. (bl) dmac/Alamy. (c) Artville. (br) Artville. **164** (tl) Brand X/Corbis. (tl) Artville. (c) Artville. (bl) Artville. (c) Alan Schein Photography/CORBIS. (tr) Artville. (cr) Ilene MacDonald/Alamy. (br) dmac/Alamy. (br) Visions of America, LLC/Alamy. **165** (tr) Paddy McGuinness/Alamy. (tl) Artville. (c) Artville. (c) Ilene MacDonald/Alamy. (bl) Visions of America, LLC/Alamy. (tr) Artville. (tr) Artville. (c) dmac/Alamy. (br) Artville. **166** (tr) BananaStock/Jupiterimages. (tl) Insy Shah/Getty Images. (c) Artville. (cl) iStockphoto.com/Justin Horrocks. (cr) Andres Rodriguez/Alamy. (bl) David Young-Wolff/PhotoEdit. (br) Jupiterimages. (c) Artville. (c) PhotoObjects.net/Jupiterimages. **167** iStockphoto.com/Matej Michelizza. (tc) iStockphoto.com/Juanmonino. (b) Blend Images/Alamy. **168** (tr) NGSP. **169** (bkgd) NGSP. **170** (br) FoodCollection/StockFood America. (cr) Masterfile (Royalty-Free Div.) **172.** (bl) JUPITERIMAGES/BananaStock/Alamy. (tl) Redchopsticks/Getty Images. (tr) tdoes/Fotolia. (br) Olga Besnard/Fotolia. (br) iStockphoto.com/RobHadfield. **172-173.** (r) Radius Images/Corbis. **174** (br) Jose Luis Pelaez, Inc/Blend Images/Jupiterimages.com. (c) Konstantin_K/Fotolia. (bl) Kris Timken/Blend Images/Jupiterimages. **175** (tl) Tomi/PhotoLink/Getty Images. (tl) Liz Garza Williams/John Paul Endress. (cl) Keith Brofsky/Getty Images. (bl) Bill Aron/PhotoEdit. (bl) Susan Van Etten/PhotoEdit. (tr) Artville. (tr) Liz Garza Williams. (cr) Kayte

Deioma/PhotoEdit. (br) Visions of America, LLC/Alamy. (br) Liz Garza Williams. (tl) Liz Garza Williams/John Paul Endress. (tl) Tomi/PhotoLink/Getty Images. (cl) Bill Aron/PhotoEdit. (bl) Susan Van Etten/PhotoEdit. (tr) Liz Garza Williams. (cr) Kayte Deioma/PhotoEdit. (br) Visions of America, LLC/Alamy. (br) Liz Garza Williams **177.** (tl) iStockphoto.com/Dmitry Mordolff. (c) 2008 © Vasily Kozlov. Image from BigStockPhoto.com. **180.** (c) Jose Luis Pelaez, Inc./Corbis. (cl) Michael Newman/PhotoEdit. (tr) Andersen Ross/Photo Library. (br) Bob Daemmrich/PhotoEdit. (bcl) B.A.E. Inc./Alamy. (bc) Pixland/Corbis. (tcr) Artville. (tcr) Image Source/Corbis. (br) Liz Garza Williams. **181** (tl) Bill Aron/PhotoEdit. (tc) Liz Garza Williams. (c) Luminis/Alamy. (tr) epantha/Fotolia. (cr) PictureLake/Fotolia. (br) Scott B. Rosen/BSG/NGSP. **182** (tl) PhotoDisc/Getty Images. (cl) PhotoDisc/Getty Images. (br) Jason Stitt/Fotolia. (bl) PhotoDisc/Getty Images. (tc) Blend Images/Alamy. **183** (cl) PhotoDisc/GettyImages. (cl) Liz Garza Williams. (bl) broker/Fotolia. (tc) pablo_hernan/Fotolia. (c) Keith Brofsky/Getty Images. (br) Bill Aron/PhotoEdit. (tr) Cone 6 Productions/Brand X/Corbis. (cr) tdoes/Fotolia. (br) Liz Garza Williams. **184** (l) 2006 © Jason Stitt. Image from BigStockPhoto.com. (r) Corbis/Jupiterimages. **185** (tl) Lugers/Fotolia. (tl) 2005 © Anne Kitzman. Image from BigStockPhoto.com. (cl) 2009 © Dmitriy Melnikov. Image from BigStockPhoto.com. (bl) iStockphoto.com/Krzysztof Rafał Siekielski. (b) Stockbyte/Getty Images. (tr) 2008 © Oleg Saenko. Image from BigStockPhoto.com. (tr) 2006 © Kevin Geary. Image from BigStockPhoto.com. (cr) iStockphoto.com/Viktor Gmyria. (br) 2006 © Ken Hurst. Image from BigStockPhoto.com. (br) 2008 © Elena Schweitzer. Image from BigStockPhoto.com **187.** (c) 2008 © Nolte Lourens. Image from BigStockPhoto.com. (tr) N M/Fotolia. (cr) Corbis Premium RF/Alamy. (tl) 2008 © Yuriy Panyukov. Image from BigStockPhoto.com. **188** (tr) Jeff Greenberg/Alamy. (tc) Teeana Williams - Fotolia.com. (b) Nancy Ney/Corbis. (tl) Enigmatico/Fotolia. **189** (bl) Scott B. Rosen. (tr) Bob Daemmrich/The Image Works. (tl) Hill Street Studios/Blend Images/Jupiterimages. (cl) Monkey Business/Fotolia. **190** (tl) Jaume Gual/age fotostock. (bl) 2008 © Chance Agrella. Image from BigStockPhoto.com. (br) Grain Belt Pictures/Alamy. (bcl) 2006 © Georgios Alexandris. Image from BigStockPhoto.com. (br) Adam Gryko/Fotolia. **191** (tl) iStockphoto.com/blaneyphoto. (cl) Digital Vision Ltd./SuperStock. (bcl) JUPITERIMAGES/Brand X /Alamy. (tr) zefa/Corbis/Jupiterimages. (br) Elvele Images Ltd/Alamy. (bcr) 2005 © Kevin Britland. Image from BigStockPhoto.com. (bc) 2006 © Ken Hurst. Image from BigStockPhoto.com **194.** (cl) 2006 © Dana Bartekoske. Image from BigStockPhoto.com. (bl) UpperCut Images/Alamy. (bkgd) 2007 © Andreas Gradin. Image from BigStockPhoto.com. **195** (tl) Giles Robberts/Alamy. (cl) L. Shat/Fotolia. (bl) Image Farm/Jupiterimages. (tr) iStockphoto.com/JMWScout. (cr) josunshine/Fotolia. (br) Photos.com/Jupiterimages. (tr) iStockphoto.com/JMWScout. **196** (tl) Ed Brennan/Fotolia. (cl) 2007 © Sue Smith. Image from BigStockPhoto.com. (bl) iStockphoto.com/Andrew Johnson. (br) GJS/Fotolia. **197** (tl) Fotolia V/Fotolia. (tc) Rob Byron/Fotolia. (tr) 2008 © Anthony Berenyi. Image from BigStockPhoto.com. (cl) Shaffer-Smith/Photo Library. (bl) David Young-Wolff/PhotoEdit. (cr) Image Farm/Jupiterimages. **198** (tr) Bill Losh/Getty Images. (c) David Young-Wolff/PhotoEdit. (br) INSADCO Photography/Alamy. (br) Jim West/Alamy. **199** (tc) Ed Brennan/Fotolia. (tr) 2007 © Harris Shiffman. Image from BigStockPhoto.com. (tl) Photos.com/Hemera Technologies/Jupiterimages. (bc) Andres Rodriguez/Fotolia. **200** (c) iStockphoto.com/Jan Rysavy. **204** (br) Somos Images LLC/Alamy. (tl) moodboard/Corbis. **204-205** (r) Galina Barskaya/Fotolia. **205** (r) iStockphoto.com/Jennifer Trenchard. (bkgd br) iStockphoto.com/Cheryl Casey. **206** (cl) Photos.com/Jupiterimages. (bl) Paul Hakimata/Fotolia. (bcl) Redchopsticks LLC/Alamy. (bc) PhotoDisc/Getty Images. (cr) Lorelyn Medina/Fotolia. (br) Edward White/Fotolia. **207** (tl) Vladimir Wrangel/Fotolia. (tcl) Creatas Images/Jupiterimages. (cl) FlemishDreams/Fotolia. (bcl) Galina Barskaya/Alamy. (bl) ImageState Royalty Free/Alamy. (tr) 2008 © Stephen Coburn. Image from BigStockPhoto.com. (tcr) Image Source/Jupiterimages. (cr) Lorelyn Medina/Fotolia. (bcr) Andres Rodriguez/Fotolia. (br) liquidlibrary/Jupiterimages. (bkgd) 2006 © Sam Aronov. Image from BigStockPhoto.com. **208** (tr) Vladimir Wrangel/Fotolia. (tcr) Creatas Images/Jupiterimages. (cr) FlemishDreams/Fotolia. (bcr) Galina Barskaya/Alamy. (br) ImageState Royalty Free/Alamy. (tl) 2008 © Stephen Coburn. Image from BigStockPhoto.com. (tcl) Image Source/Jupiterimages. (cl) Lorelyn Medina/Fotolia. (bcl) Andres Rodriguez/Fotolia. (bl) liquidlibrary/Jupiterimages. (br) 2007 © Andreas Gradin. Image from BigStockPhoto.com. (br) 2007 © Andreas Gradin. Image from BigStockPhoto.com. (bkgd) 2006 © Sam Aronov. Image from BigStockPhoto.com. **209** (tl) 2008 © Cathy Yeulet. Image from BigStockPhoto.com. (tr) 2006 © Andres Rodriguez. Image from BigStockPhoto.com. (tc) Gary Salter/zefa/Corbis. (cl) sparkmom/Fotolia. (bl) iStockphoto.com/Kevin Russ. (cr) 2008 © Radu Razvan. Image from BigStockPhoto.com. (c) 2005 © Karen Struthers. Image from BigStockPhoto.com. **210** (cl) Comstock Images/